PETERHEAD

PETERHEAD

The Inside Story of Scotland's Toughest Prison

Robert Jeffrey

BLACK & WHITE PUBLISHING

First published 2013
by Black & White Publishing Ltd
29 Ocean Drive, Edinburgh EH6 6JL

3 5 7 9 10 8 6 4 2   15 16 17 18

ISBN: 978 1 84502 538 0

A CIP catalogue record for this book is available from the British Library.

Typeset by Iolaire Typesetting, Newtonmore
Printed and bound by Grafica Veneta S.p.A Italy

CONTENTS

ACKNOWLEDGEMENTS

The author would like to thank the following for their help with this book: The staff of the National Archives in Edinburgh and the Mitchell Library in Glasgow, Ronnie Brownie, Jessica Bird, Stuart Campbell, Willie "Sonny" Leitch, Dr Grant Jeffrey, Dr Stuart Jeffrey, Walter Norval, Mandy Rhodes, *Holyrood* magazine, Tom Fox, Ruth Wishart, James Crosbie, Albert Whyte, Mike Hebden, Derek McGill, Mary Stewart, Graeme Smith, Kirsty Gibbins and many prison officers who served in Peterhead, as well as sundry prisoners who did time "up north."

1

ICY SEAS, ICY CELLS AND BREAKING ROCKS

To a miserable wretch of a prisoner in the new Peterhead Prison, just opened in 1888, there was one maritime connection that few would have realised. Remarkably, the reason why the lawbreakers – a few hundred in the early days – were incarcerated in this particular area in the North-East of Scotland, on the edge of the turbulent waters of the North Sea, surrounded by howling winds, slanting snow and sleet and mighty breakers, had much to do with the habits of the whale. The giant cetaceans were breeding and feeding in the icy waters around Greenland, and in the later part of the nineteenth century the hard-as-nails east coast fishermen from both north and south of the Scottish border took to the seas to chase and catch these gentle giants of the deep and take meat and oil from them south. Particularly to Peterhead and Hull, where men grew rich on the, at that time, seemingly endless supply of mammals to be harvested for that now largely forgotten but once valuable commodity – whale oil. The oil was valuable for the production of candle wax, soap and margarine, and whalebone too had its uses in spectacle frames and corsets, amongst other items.

Like "big oil," which was to come to the North-East of Scotland around a hundred years later, whaling was a highly profitable enterprise. In the same way as today a spell "on the rigs" attracts adventurers, a voyage on a whaler was something of a rite of passage for young men making their way in the world. Sir Arthur Conan Doyle, creator of Sherlock Holmes, was one of those who succumbed to the lure of the north when studying medicine in Edinburgh. In the late 1880s he joined the crew of a three-master called *Hope* as ship's surgeon, and headed north. In his diaries on the voyage he noted his surprise at how close to the doorstep of Peterhead lay the dangers and wealth of the Greenland seas. A mere four days north of Shetland and you were amid the ice floes and in the home waters of the giant whales. Scottish whalers also took the rather longer voyage south to Antarctica in search of whale oil.

The trade of fishing and whaling was a dangerous one, not just in the northern oceans but in the North Sea itself. Many whalers lost their lives in such wild waters. And shipping disasters in the Aberdeenshire area were not confined to whale hunters – there were many other sea tragedies involving fishing vessels and ships trading around Britain and the continent, as well as smaller coasters running up and down to the east coast, who fell victim to the spectacular but dangerous rocks and hidden reefs in the area – especially in the violent storms and troublesome North Sea *haars* that could cut visibility to a matter of yards and bedevilled navigators before the days of radar and global positioning satellites. The problem was big enough to involve both the government of the time and any lay person with an interest in safety at sea. Apart from the whalers, the cargo ships and the fishing fleets, the Admiralty also had a vested interest in the well-being of their warships going about the business of Britannia ruling the waves.

The danger to life is well illustrated by the fact that in 1890 Peterhead's fishing fleet numbered almost 600 vessels. At first the main catch was herring but as the stocks of this popular and tasty fish declined, the switch was made to other white fish. In 1887 around 120,000 tons of fish were landed at Peterhead, by then the biggest fish market in Europe. It was a massive industry with, before and after the First World War, several fish trains leaving the area daily, taking supplies to the prosperous and densely populated areas in London and the south east of England, where citizens with money to spare and living far from the sea had developed a taste for fresh seafood.

On the safety at sea issue the main problem was that in an onshore gale there were few safe harbours for the large ships of the time – sail as well as steam – to run to for shelter. But gradually in high places in the government and in commerce, a solution came to mind: build what was known as a Harbour of Refuge. Not a commercial collection of piers and wharves, but an area where the violent force of the ocean winds and seas were tamed by huge encircling breakwaters, a place where civilian ships, fishing boats and whalers and even the Royal Navy's warships could run to for shelter in the wildest of weather and lie in peace and safety till the storms abated. It was clear that at the time there was no such place on the east coast, so an ambitious, indeed daring, plan to build what was in effect a giant lagoon at Peterhead, popularly known as the "Blue Toon" – a nickname that sprang from the colour of the local fishermen's thick woollen socks – took firm hold on the public imagination as well as that of seafarers.

The early research showed that to build such a place you needed a ready access to stone for the giant blocks required to hold back the waves. And, above all, in the days before mechanical devices were in ready supply, you needed massive amounts of manual labour both to quarry the stone and to build the sea walls – and that was costly even back then. However, of all the east coast alternatives, the boffins of the day decided that Peterhead was the best spot for the Harbour of Refuge. There was plenty of stone around, but the locals in the thriving whaling and fishing town surrounded by prosperous farming lands were making good livings and were unlikely to want to become harbour builders. But there was another way: convict labour. It had been used with great success for harbours in England. The main problem, however, was that there was no prison anywhere near the proposed Aberdeenshire site.

The answer was, as they say nowadays, a no-brainer. Simply build a new prison. This would also serve another purpose. At this time many Scottish convicts, particularly those who had committed really serious crimes, were sent south of the border to serve their time, such was the lack of prisons in Scotland. So a new Scottish prison was an attractive prospect to the authorities on several grounds. As far back as 1881 a Committee on the Employment of Convicts reported "that the most likely prospect for benefitting the shipping and fishery interest of the country at large, and at the same time profitably employing convicts, is the construction of a Harbour of Refuge at Peterhead in Aberdeenshire."

However, the years before the opening of the prison were fraught with many problems, including finance, and it was to be a further seven years before the first Glasgow convicts were to arrive north to spend their days and nights in a massive granite fortress that was to become, in time, the most infamous jail in the land.

The Peterhead Harbour of Refuge Act had gone through the Commons in 1886 and put the Admiralty in charge of the huge construction job of creating the massive breakwaters needed for the desired safe haven for shipping. The site was on a promontory near Salthouse Head at the southern end of Peterhead Bay, some thirty-four miles north of Aberdeen.

The Prison Commissioners had their own problems building and opening the new prison that was to be the home for the convict labour that was to build the harbour. Some thousands of pounds to pay for the early part of the building project had been released by the government at the time of the passing of the Act, and on 11 March 1886 the release of the cash was publicly announced. But a mere two days later there was some embarrassment for the Commissioners, who had to write to the Under Secretary of State to say that the Paymaster General "has not sufficient money on the vote for Prisons, Scotland, to carry out the transfer and have been requested by him [the Paymaster General] to arrange for the payment through their account with the Queen's and Lord Treasurer's Remembrancer." The usual civil service bean counters shuffling papers and creating problems! Nothing new there then. But the money was found soon enough.

There was another significant development in the run up to the opening in August 1888. The government deemed that the new prison would be a "general" prison rather than an "ordinary" prison. This may seem like semantics, but it did have one effect that impinged on the treatment of prisoners. The Prison Commissioners were moved to point out that "section 14 of the Prisons Act provides for the appointment of visiting committees to Ordinary Prisons and that as a General Prison it will not be competent to appoint a visiting committee to Peterhead but that powers of visitation are vested in Sheriffs and Justices under section 16 of the Prison Act and that special visitors may be appointed as in the case of English convict prisons." Any cruelty or wrongdoing in the way prisoners were held was therefore going to be much harder to control. The place that was to become Scotland's toughest prison was, it seemed, starting the way it was to go on.

This reference to the English penal system is another example of the way prisons in Scotland were run in the nineteenth century – the authorities were obsessed with what happened south of the border and seemed desperate to integrate their thinking with that of the English. The edict on visiting might seem on the face of it a small point, but visiting committees have been an enormous force for good, right to the present day. In the mind of any governor, any prison officer and any prisoner with a grievance, the thought of douce, well-meaning citizens turning up regularly, to visit and to inspect prison practices and the well-being of the incarcerated, concentrates the mind in a positive way. It was also an early example of trying to integrate prisons and their local communities, a concept that is now growing in popularity.

Apart from the prison plans, the Harbour of Refuge Act dealt in some detail with the task faced by both engineers and the convicts in its construction, starting with: "A breakwater pier is to be constructed at or near the reclaimed land at Keith Inch Island." It was thence to proceed in a south-westerly direction for a distance of thousands of feet. A retaining "wall or quay" was also to be built "starting from the north-west side of the previously mentioned breakwater starting eighty yards or so from the first breakwater." This was to head for about "one hundred and seventeen yards to the north-west corner of the reclaimed land." Another breakwater pier was to be built "about seventeen yards, or thereabouts, eastward of the property at Salthouse Head known as St Catherine's."

You can almost hear the scratch of pen on parchment in this description of the work involved in creating the Harbour of Refuge. But there was no underestimating the difficulty and complexity of this engineering project designed to save the lives of those who plied the seas in search of whale, white fish or to engage in trade. The hapless early inhabitants of Peterhead Prison itself had years of hard labour vividly sketched out for them by the Parliamentary scribes.

Apart from the obvious effect on the seafront, the project was to cause major changes, even inland. New roads were to be built and a railway constructed to connect a quarry, the prison and the construction yard at the harbour. The railway was to run from St Catherine's to terminate at the quarry, and the Admiralty was given more or less *carte blanche* to move houses and existing tracks and road as part of the master plan. These days local objectors would no doubt hold back such a building project for years with endless expensive inquiries that would make many lawyers rich, but in less sophisticated days that was not a problem.

Little matters like consultation with locals affected by the project were not to be allowed to slow construction. In particular the holder of the office of harbourmaster was given more or less dictator status in the collection of dues and running the building sites around the harbour. This was important stuff, and although the actual building work had started, the final authorisation of the harbour/prison/

quarry/railway appeared in the *Edinburgh Gazette* of 29 June 1888 – along with such other titbits of information such as that Mr John Galloway was to be Consul General at Glasgow for the Republic of Paraguay and that Maharaja Narendra Krishna deb Bahadur was appointed Knight Commander of the Eminent Order of the Indian Empire. As they used to say of the late unlamented *News of the World* – "all the news that's fit to print"!

The notion of building a Harbour of Refuge had been talked about as far back as 1859 and in fact work on the breakwater started in 1886 and was supposed to last for twenty-five years. But it continued, interrupted by two World Wars, until the final few granite blocks were laid in the late 1950s.

As previously noted, in the early days a letter from the Treasury recommended to those concerned with the project that the south bay at Peterhead was the best choice for the site. There was more detail: "Principally on the grounds that the construction proposal for the works is peculiarly suitable to convict labour." Peterhead was judged "the place capable of affording the maximum shelter, the necessity of which can be foreseen, or that can reasonably be required, under all conditions of wind and weather, for passing ships engaged in commerce, together with space available of a few cruisers of the Royal Navy. And also to give accommodation to the fleets of fishing boats occasionally congregated on this line of the coast." The throwaway line on a "few" cruisers raises an eyebrow in these modern days when the Navy has, sadly, more captains than ships.

From the beginning, the link between the prison and the imaginative and massive humanitarian civil engineering project was vital. The authorities were also concerned with the long-term and wanted the prison built in a way that would allow it to be expanded and used as a place of incarceration after the harbour was up and running. The fact that when North Sea oil began to be extracted in a hundred or so years' time the sheltered harbour would suck big oil money into the area was, of course, an unforeseen and lucky twist of fate.

Even in the far-off days when the new project was started you never got anywhere without a committee. So one was formed with the interested parties being the Home Office, the Admiralty Department of Engineers and Architectural Works, the Board of Trade, the Prison Commission of Scotland plus a nominated member of the Merchant Company of Edinburgh who had control of lands in and around Peterhead. The old joke about a committee being an organisation that takes minutes and wastes hours comes to mind. But they got it done. The Harbour of Refuge was to become fact rather than a dream.

Life in Peterhead prison was for the convicts, from day one to those imprisoned at closure in the far-off twenty-first century, to be earthy about it – pure "shit". So any complaining cons might have had a laugh at the early reports on buying the farmland for the site of the prison. The land was controlled by the august Merchant Company of Edinburgh. The committee in charge of the project was concerned that a "fair" price was paid to the farmers and that there was to be a feu duty which should "include the value of the crops and unexhausted manure"! The farms involved were Middleton of Clerkhill and Wellington and to begin with the area was around twenty-five acres. Sir John Coode was engineer in chief and a Major Beamish of the Royal Engineers was architect to the Prison Commissioners. No doubt the farmers were happy to sell, as the land could no doubt have been obtained by compulsory purchase. What happened to that "exhausted manure" remains a mystery.

One of the first tasks facing those running the project was to choose a quarry. Delegations of bigwigs had a look at three quarries and there was no shortage of granite or quarries in the area. First to be looked at was the Upper Quarry at Stirling Hill, three miles north of the harbour site, then Blackhill, a half mile closer, then finally Boddam. Stirling Hill granite was used in many of London's most notable buildings, including Australia House and Covent Garden, and some even found its way into public buildings in Canada. At one time there had been almost a dozen quarries in the area. The granite that came from them was considered to be suitable to withstand the pounding of the North Sea for centuries and here in the huge quarries the convicts who would smash rocks were offered a choice of seven- or fourteen-pound hammers. Those who swung such muscle-breaking implements would no doubt be unimpressed that in earlier times, four thousand years ago, ancient man in the Neolithic age had formed flint into hunting tools in encampments near to this site. Nor, I suspect, would they much care that the granite they were attacking with the sledgehammers had started life as a molten layer five kilometres down millions of years ago. But if the cons ever did think about the material they were working with, it certainly would have put a sentence of a few years in jail into perspective!

A major practical advantage of quarrying in the area with convicts was the closeness of the sea, which was particularly important, as it blocked any escapes on the east of the prison except for the most determined. As we will see later, escapers down the years, like the legendary Johnny

Ramensky and others, were forced into fairly heavily populated countryside immediately after they had got over the
prison wall unseen by the guards, something that made the
detection of a fleeing convict that much easier. The escape
routes were limited. The site for the prison also had the
advantage that it was near the town water and gas supply
and had good road connections with Aberdeen.

The quarry site was also vital. Consider the plans for a
breakwater to be built largely by manual labour: First a
"kind of embankment" fifty feet high was to be built in the
sea, then on top of that five- or six-feet-high blocks of stone
were put down. And on top of that huge concrete blocks
made of granite crushed at the Admiralty site were added.
Some blocks were said to be up to forty feet high. It might
look to the layman like over specification, but not if you
have seen North Sea rollers in a winter gale.

The rough state of the seas also came into play when the
problem of moving the granite from quarry to harbour site
had to be resolved. Initially it seemed that using barges
might be a good idea. And the barges could perhaps also
transfer prisoners from jail to the harbour work shed. But
on consideration there were deemed to be important snags
with this idea – not least the thought of convicts desperate
to escape taking hostages and seizing control of the barges.
Also, work would be confined to spells of decent weather.
And the alternative of marching men between quarry,
harbour and the prison did not seem too clever either.

It may have been what we now call "blue sky" thinking
but a railway was by far the best solution to a unique
set of problems. The fact that some of the blocks needed
were too big to be transported by a mini railway did not
matter – they could be built in work sheds at the harbour

11

from stone broken by convicts swinging sledgehammers up at the quarry. And convicts could "commute" from the prison to the quarry and to the harbour on the rail line. Sand and gravel were also available in plentiful quantities at the seashore. The railway was unique in that it was the only state-owned passenger-carrying line in its day. Just a few miles long, but a nationalised railway nonetheless.

So the rough outline of the procedures involved in the project had been established. The cost of the prison was, seemingly like every building estimate since the first brick was laid on brick, rising. Early estimates were an optimistic £43,000 or so. But when detailed work was done on the plans it seemed like more than £90,000 was needed. (Interestingly, the prison's twenty-first century replacement, HMP Grampian, is costed at more than £140 million and take no bets on that figure not rising.) The architects were sent back to the drawing boards to think again. Money had to be saved. This they did by cutting back on staff quarters, using less stone on walls in and around the grounds and substituting corrugated iron for slate on some roofs. A hard-hearted suggestion that savings could be made by providing dry earth toilets for the prisoners rather than water closets was rejected. The cost came down to around £56,000. And the doors did open. Or clanged loudly behind you if you were a lawbreaker. That was not the end of building work, though, and additional structures were erected in 1909, 1960 and 1962.

When the breakwater was conceived, the long term, as opposed to the early building costs, of the undertaking was estimated at £750,000, it being anticipated that the work would be completed in twenty-five years. But from the arrival of the first convict it was to be more than seventy years before the last granite block was laid in the north breakwater.

From 1888 the harbour facilities were gradually improved with the building of the huge breakwaters that were creeping slowly out from the shore, the largest being 900m in length. As this work went on, the boom and bust in the whaling industry was beginning to be mirrored in the herring fishery. Though even the slimmed-down fishery still had one of the biggest fish markets in Europe, with herring largely replaced by other species. Over recent years the difficulties in the fishing industry, the downsizing of the RAF presence in the area and uncertainty about the future of the prison itself have caused some worry in the local business community. But, of course, since the 1970s Peterhead prison has been an important part of the North Sea oil industry, something that brought unexpected wealth to the area. And now with the new HMP Grampian under construction to replace both the town's old Victorian jail and Craiginches in Aberdeen, the town and surrounding countryside has an air of prosperity.

But all this bustle and boom was far in the future when, even in the nineteenth century, Peterhead Prison was starting to earn a reputation as the toughest prison in the country. Conditions there were harsh even for the time. One local paper commented with masterly understatement that the accommodation in the cells is "limited" and went on to describe a cell. It pointed out that all the cells were identical from basement to top storey. Each cell was seven feet by five feet and only nine feet high. Originally there were 208 in a block. The only natural light came from an eighteen-inch square window with strong steel frames and iron stanchions on the outside built into the granite wall. On top of "each door is an iron box with flaps for ventilation. Each cell was lighted at night by a single gas jet enclosed in an iron box inaccessible to the prisoner." This report went on again with that same understatement to say that the fittings are "very limited" and comprised of a small hinged flap of iron covered in wood which was used as the "poor" convict's table. The size of this table was two feet by eighteen inches. The sleeping accommodation was a hammock slung on hooks at each end of the cell. The report went on to remark that this was the sole furniture in the cell.

Those tiny cells in the hellish prison were, over the years, to be a second home for the low-lifers of the Glasgow streets. A spell in Peterhead was almost a necessity if you wanted to claw your way to the top of the crime ladder in Scotland's industrial capital. In May 1888 the *Aberdeen Journal* reported on the start of what was to become an almost traditional journey for Glasgow's bad guys. The prison was due to open for business in July/August of that year and at the Glasgow Circuit Court twenty-one men were sentenced to penal servitude for various crimes. They were to do their time in the new prison. At the trial Lord Young had expressed his desire to rid the city of "dangerous characters whose sole aim and object in life was to prey on society." The *Journal* went on to say: "there was a slight commotion at Buchanan Street station as the prison van – better known to its occupants as the Black Maria – rolled into the railway station where there was a posse of police in attendance." According to the report, a smart warder opened the doors of the van and the curiosity of friends and passengers was satisfied. Twenty-one "powerful-looking men dressed in moleskin and caps, stamped with a broad arrow, stepped on to the platform. The convicts were handcuffed and linked to a strong chain that made escape out of the question."

It was said that the men who filed into the railway van provided for them looked like men capable of doing good service in the public works at Peterhead Prison "which is now ready for their reception." It was then explained to the readers that at the prison "the civil guards with loaded rifles will command the heights above the quarries and commanding positions in the vicinity of the prison." Reportage slipped into comment at the end of the article: "One sad feature is the extreme youth of many of this gang, their ages not exceeding twenty. There is no doubt the city is well rid of them."

The curiosity of the public to see the villains bound for Peterhead was not confined to Glasgow. A special railway Black Maria – the only one of its kind in the country – was met at Peterhead with crowds of locals bent on catching a glimpse of the men who were to be the first of many thousands who would spend their days and nights behind bars in misery in what would in time become Scotland's most infamous and toughest jail.

The original accommodation, which was completed by about 1889, was for 208 prisoners. In the early years of the twentieth century the numbers held fluctuated considerably. The average was around 350, though there was a peak of 455 in 1911. These figures are not impressive compared to other famous jails in Britain and round the world. But there is a Scottish saying that "guid gear gangs in sma bulk" – maybe in the case of Peterhead the world "guid" could be substituted with three others, "misery, deprivation and violence."

2

A RAILWAY, RIFLES AND A
CAT O' NINE TALES

The argument on what prison is for rages on today, many years after the opening of Peterhead – is it revenge, retribution or redemption? There are still those who believe in throwing away the key, just as there are still those who thirst for the return of the rope. There is no final answer to the debate. Peterhead and Barlinnie are the two most famous places of incarceration in Scotland but there is a dramatic difference in the forces that led to the building of each prison. Peterhead, as we have seen, grew out of ideas far removed from prison reform. Safety at sea was paramount here. It was rather different in the case of the Bar-L down in the altogether far rougher environs of the east end of Glasgow.

In the city there was an early body of humanitarian laymen and women who wanted to improve the conditions in which convicts were held – so at least the two prisons were linked to some extent by humanitarian good intentions. In Peterhead it was the creation of that Harbour of Refuge, in Glasgow it was to ameliorate the horrific conditions prisoners were held in in the existing prisons in this hard city. In Glasgow the good intentions that helped create Barlinnie were of little avail – the place was overcrowded virtually from day one. Peterhead never really suffered from such chronic overcrowding but, as we will see as its history unfolds, it became a far worse place of confinement than its big brother down south.

Firearms were one of the biggest differences in the two jails. They don't feature much in the Barlinnie story but they are an integral part of the history of Peterhead. It is easy to see why – Barlinnie prisoners were seldom let out from behind the walls but in Peterhead cons had to be moved around outside the prison on a regular basis to do the work of building the harbour. So guns of all sorts are deeply folded into the Peterhead story.

In addition to the complication of moving prisoners about outside the prison there was the added danger that the place was intended to hold in custody the toughest of the tough in Scotland. It was the home of those serving the longest sentences. This at the time when violence was commonplace and where, in the stews of the big cities, ordinary folk often walked in fear of attack from gang members or simply worried about the threat of dangerous rascals bent on highway robbery, bank robbery or burglary. Razor slashers were no newspaper fantasy. Knives were popular and to be "tooled up" was an everyday fact of life for the big-timers, especially in Glasgow which was home – if you could call it that – to most of the denizens of the bleak cells of Peterhead.

For the folk who ran the place from day one there was an imperative: ensure as far as possible the safety of warders, as well as that of the good folk who lived in the town and farmlands nearby. The convicts were mostly conscienceless men who lived a life of violence. The politicians and planners in Edinburgh and local bigwigs in the North-East, as well as the existing prison authorities, were well aware of the potential for mass violence in such a remote jail where the inhabitants were hand-picked bad guys who would have created trouble anywhere they found themselves. This was long before Hollywood would turn films of the 'Riot in Cell Block "B"' style into an entertainment staple – and the days of the tabloids splashing stories of cons breaking out on to prison roofs and capturing hostages, as well as showering their captors with stones and slates, were more than fifty years into the future. But the danger in the job was recognised.

Right from the start, Peterhead warders were issued with a cutlass and scabbard as part of the uniform and they were encouraged to draw the weapons whenever they felt even slightly threatened. To an unarmed man a crack across the chest with a sword blade was a considerable disincentive to misbehaviour, and the warders knew it. The blades were no ornamental comic opera pieces of weaponry. No style statement. They were used to prod and whack the guys whenever there was the slightest need. The swords were effective weapons of control in a harsh prison regime. There is no record of Errol Flynn-style sword fights, all flashing blades and men in fancy tights leaping about. But if no prisoners had their guts rearranged by a sword thrust, plenty had a whack on the head or shoulders from the side of a blade. When a warder drew his sword, a con paid attention.

As the work goes on in preparing for the eventual complete destruction of the old prison and a transfer to the new HMP Grampian being constructed nearby, the staff have been gathering together all sorts of memorabilia and in the course of this search one of the old swords has been found and in brand-new condition. It is an impressive piece of equipment, both as a beautiful example of the sword makers' art and a valuable weapon for the prison officers. The swords ceased to be part of the prison officers' weaponry in 1939 and this particular example, currently held in the prison, is well worth its place in any museum of criminology. A rifle is, of course, a more deadly weapon and Lee Enfields were carried until as late as 1959, when they were generally replaced with less threatening batons.

Intriguingly, one famous 1930s riot in Barlinnie was put down by use of batons rather than sword or rifles and many prisoners were injured before peace was restored to Glasgow's Big Hoose in the east end. Naturally a court of inquiry was convened into the events, known as the Tobacco Riots, and one of the most important findings was that a heavier baton was needed by the warders since so many had broken too easily when battered against the skulls of the rioters. This might say something of the strength of the skull of a Glasgow hard man as well as the manufacturer of the batons!

Prison riots were inevitable and they could be short-lived outbreaks with the warders outfighting inmates or, as we see later, full-scale wars between captives and captors that could last for days on end. Peterhead was to have its moments in the history of prison riots in the years ahead.

The early weapons authorised by the Secretary of State for use by warders in case of attack by prisoners, or to prevent any escape, were firearms with shot cartridges. But the real fear of the prisoners turning on their guards played a role in the creation of a now largely forgotten piece of Scottish prison history – the previously mentioned Peterhead private railway. All the pieces were in place for the building of the Harbour of Refuge. The Admiralty engineers and planners were there. The stone from the quarry was there. The workforce of prisoners was there. But quarry, prison and harbour were miles apart. In particular there was the problem of security as the prisoners had to be out of the prison to work and they had to move under guard around the three sites. Much thought had to go into how this was to be done. The initial idea was to march the workforce to where it was needed with armed warders in charge. Another idea, as earlier mentioned, was to take prisoners by sea using barges to get to the harbour, but this was quickly abandoned as it was clear the winter weather (and often summer!) meant that this would be a dangerous process. The marching of desperadoes around the country did not have much appeal either, especially if it meant a handful of warders in charge of dozens of prisoners. The chances of a mass breakout were high and lives could have been lost. To move the prisoners around in this way would not have appealed to the locals either. An altogether more practical solution was the train line between the three sites. In compartments on the moving train the guards would have much more control and so a line unique in railway history came to be built.

Today there is little sign of it – traces of the odd bridge, overgrown cuttings and little else. The dedicated backpacker in stout boots and armed with a good map can find a few traces of this remarkable line, but anyone else on the wander in the area of the prison and the harbour, or the quarry, will see little sign of it. One exception is on the hill just outside the prison on the main road to Aberdeen. Travelling south just before the Stirling Hill Quarry there are some stone structures still visible, pillars of a bridge that helped the railway cross the road. The modern traveller will glance at it without an awareness of its history. But it is hard to miss.

Steam and railways have a fascination for many folk and obscure little lines are well documented in the railway press and some are even preserved by enthusiasts who are never happier than wiping an oily rag on overalls and breathing in the less than healthy smoke of a steam engine, not to mention the ashes and hot grime that sinks into clothing. What a pity that this unique railway was not preserved; it would have made a wonderful tourist attraction.

There are few alive who remember riding on it either as convicts or guards, but there is a wonderful little word picture of it that was published in *The Locomotive Magazine* in 1900. The line was only a couple of miles or so long but was described by the magazine as "A British State Railway." The railway ran between the quarry of Stirling Hill, the prison, the harbour and the breakwater construction site; the breakwater was said at the time to be the largest in the world. It is worth recording what the magazine had to say about this part of the construction of a Harbour of Refuge. The writer of the article declaimed:

When the British government undertake any work one may as a rule depend upon that work being well done, so to convey the convicts to and from the quarries and the granite to the break-water an elaborate little railway has been constructed. Although the total length of the line is but two and a half miles yet the whole works are of the most elaborate construction. Heavy flat-bottomed rails weighing about 72lb per yard and spiked to the sleepers in the ordinary manner form the permanent way which is firmly and compactly ballasted with granite. The line

21

contains some engineering works of a fair size, including a massive viaduct of several spans of granite, masonry, a steel girder bridge across the turnpike road, two masonry overbridges and heavy cuttings and embankments. In general equipment, too, this railway is fully equal to a trunk line, being provided with a complete signalling system, all trains being worked on the absolute block from three cabins in electrical contact with each other.

It went on to describe how the passenger train service consisted of two trains in each direction daily to take convicts and officers travelling to their work outside the prison walls. These trains left the Admiralty Station Peterhead at 7.15am and 1pm and from Stirling Hill at 11am and 5pm. Other "mineral trains" were run as required to move the blocks of granite to the various sites. The passenger stock comprised of four corridor cars.

Despite what the magazine article called the elaborate construction of the line, this was obviously no *Orient Express*. The coaches were of substantial construction and were *"more remarkable for utility than comfort."* They had six windowless compartments though there were windows on the side doors. Each coach could take around thirty-five passengers and 100 could be carried on each train. There were four engines of the *Thomas the Tank* style any child could recognise – Victoria (1892); Prince of Wales (1892), Alexandra (1892), all built in Leeds; and Duke of York (1896), built in Newcastle. All were painted a dull olive green and had polished brass domes.

There were no liveried flunkeys handing out refreshments, but the wagon in front was used for the convenience of occasional passengers who were not to travel in the convict cars. Almost all of it is gone now though one piece of rolling stock – one of the wagons that held the convicts – is rumoured to be used to this day as a henhouse on a farm in rural Lanarkshire. That may or may not be true but in a little railway museum in Maud, a village inland in the rolling farmland behind Peterhead, there is one wagon saved from life as a henhouse. The intention is to rebuild it into the condition it was in when it was making history as part of Britain's first state railway, but though the will is there so far the cash isn't. But it is a good excuse to tarry awhile in one of Scotland's most attractive villages, and the cash deserves to be found to preserve this relic of a historic railway.

It has to be said that the trains served their purpose well and there are no records of escapes taking place when the prisoners were in transit. This is surprising since in recent years almost all jail "escapes" were actually convicts absconding from work parties or when being taken to and from courts or on transfer from one establishment to another. Every governor knows that the security weak link happens when moving prisoners around and that is when the system is most vulnerable.

No actual escapes from the prison express, it seems, but there is one tale you might still hear from some greybeard in a local pub. The yarn goes that on one occasion on arrival back at the prison the head count showed one person missing. The guards, in a panic, ran back up the tracks to find the prisoner walking along the sleepers back towards the prison – he had accidentally missed his train. At least, that is the story! It is something we have all done at one time or another. Maybe, however unlikely it sounds, he preferred tea in the jail with his mates rather than being hunted down like an animal by armed prison officers in a futile bid for freedom.

The little railway must have been the only one in the county where the staff were armed at all times. As were, of course, the staff in the prison itself. Right from the opening day the warders, as they were then, before they officially became "prison officers", were armed with both swords and firearms.

Back in the years before 1900 when the prison was building up a stock of necessary equipment, "whipping implements" were on the governor's shopping list, and the archives duly note that a cat o' nine tails and birch rods were approved for the punishment of prisoners and delivered on 24 July 1885 – even before the building work was anywhere near complete. The Scottish prisons were constantly looking over their shoulders at what was going on in England and, as a result, in December 1888 – the year the first cons arrived – four Enfield Mk2 pistols as issued south of the border were delivered. But an oversight meant that the holsters had been forgotten. A request was then sent for four leather holsters to be provided. The colour black was the preferred choice. You can't beat a touch of style.

Those who run prisons to this day love to have guidelines and detailed instructions on how to deal with the day-to-day running. Everything from the thickness of a slice of toast or how much tea is in a cuppa is detailed. When it comes to weapons, the wordsmiths who write the rules have a field day. And it was no different when Peterhead came into being. The early governors wanted the use of swords and firearms to be approved under strict rules of engagement, as they say these days. And the use of firearms or other weapons would not come as a surprise to any inmate. Right from the early days one of the rituals on arrival in the grim halls of Peterhead was to make sure the prisoners knew the score as to what would happen to them if they broke the rules. A somewhat fearsome warning was read to them on admission. It takes little imagination to think how offenders must have felt when listening to this little lecture:

> *Convicts confined in HM Prison Peterhead are hereby warned that they are liable to have swords, bayonets or rifles used against them if they attempt to escape either when inside or outside the prison or if they at any time, either singly or in combination, attack or attempt to attack or forcibly resist a prison officer.*

So now they knew! Originally, the then Secretary of State was of the opinion that officers should use firearms with shot cartridges in breakouts and attacks. Later experts deemed this as "useless or dangerous" but when the gate to new equipment officially swung open to other weapons of choice, other than the swords and bayonets, Snider carbines firing buckshot were in the frame. Buckshot wounds tended to be more serious than a single bullet aimed at a vulnerable spot, like a knee, to stop an escaper, and the longer range of a military rifle made escape more difficult, something the prisoners, many of whom had firearm experience, could understand. Rifles were also more useful in the event of an outside attack on the prison. But it was almost thirty years after the prison opened before service rifles became standard. In the 1920s ex-army rifles, which were presumably in good supply after the First World War, were loaned to the prison.

The loan period was by way of a trial but it was not long before these rifles were deemed the proper weapon for the job. It was said that: "Experience in the war (1914–1918) shows that the modern rifle with small bore bullets of high velocity is less likely to endanger life than a carbine loaded with buckshot." Interestingly, the authorities were also taking account of "the possibility of attack from the outside." In the early 1920s both Barlinnie and Peterhead had relied on extra borrowed weapons from the military in case of this contingency. The fear was that Sinn Fein would attack prisons where their men were held. Indeed, they had made threats that they would do just that. The authorities in Edinburgh gave thought to adding revolvers to the weaponry in addition to the rifles, swords and bayonets. But there was a training problem here – the warders had no experience of revolvers – the early four Enfield Mk2s seemed to be largely there to impress prisoners rather than gun them down – and this proposal was sidelined.

The weapons issue made headlines in July 1932 when a prisoner was shot dead running away from a work party and this started a legal argument on whether or not the action taken by Whyte, the guard who fired the fatal shot, was appropriate or not. An inquiry found that the officer used his rifle "in the ordinary execution of his duties and in accordance with prison regulations." The said regulations ran along these lines: "A prison officer who sees any suspicious movement on the part of any convict, or who feels doubtful about the intention of any convict, will immediately challenge the convict concerned, load his rifle, and, as may be necessary, communicate with any other prison officer within hearing, blow his whistle and give the alarm signal. If the officer is armed with a bayonet in addition to a rifle, or armed with a sword only, he will fix the bayonet or draw his sword if in his opinion it is necessary and advantageous to do so, after he has given the necessary signals." The instructions were clear: if attacked, fix bayonet, load rifle, draw sword. The weapons were only to be used inside the Admiralty yard or the prison yard if a convict tried to scale a wall or escape through an opening. Warders were instructed in using the sword or bayonet to inflict minimum damage consistent with stopping the escape. If the rifle was to be used, one or two warning shots were to be fired before taking aim.

The reference to the alarm signal is interesting. This was, of course, in the days before mobile phones or personal radios and the cons could be in the prison yard, working down at the harbour or at the quarries. And only a few officers had to keep control of work parties made up of desperate men well used to violence in their lives inside and outside the prison. The conditions in the prison, the food, the toilet facilities and the occasional cruel and conscienceless guard, the bitter North-East weather, all combined to make the prisoners gather in surly groups. Even the threat of a lick or two from the cat wielded by a sadistic officer was not a complete deterrent.

Keeping such men in line was no occupation for softies. The guards used a primitive sort of body semaphore to keep in touch with each other. Standing erect with hands above their head was the signal for a general alarm; a sort of "T" shape meant stop work; another signal meant take cover; and yet another, one arm moved up and down slowly, gave the all clear.

The prisoner who was shot by Officer Whyte was George Kynoch. As pointed out earlier, the prison officer was largely cleared, as what he had done was "not unreasonable in a serious emergency." He was deemed to have been doing his duty and it was thought by the prison and legal establishment that if proceedings had been taken against him it would have been detrimental to discipline in the prison. But it was acknowledged that the regulations were too vague, hence the guidance given above to all officers after this incident. Mind you, back in 1888 the first governor, S. A. Dodd, had said it was justified to shoot to stop an escape but not to kill. Although perhaps that's easier said than done.

3

MURDER IN THE MOUNTAINS AND DEATH IN THE QUARRY

Most folk these days if asked about Peterhead inmates will mention Jimmy Boyle, Oscar Slater or Paddy Meehan. Maybe Johnny Ramensky or Glasgow Godfathers Walter Norval and Arthur Thompson would also come to the forefront of popular memory. Or TC Campbell and Joe Steele of the Ice Cream War miscarriage of justice. But in the early years the prison held a now largely forgotten murderer with a very interesting story. This prisoner had been convicted of murder, though he may well have been innocent.

Around the turn of the last century a name linked with Peterhead and often in the headlines was that of "The Arran Murderer," as John Watson Laurie became known. Writers of fictional mystery tales often look for the perfect method of committing a murder and some turn their pens to stories of mountaineering. Imagine two men disappearing into the cloud high on a mountain where the ground is slippery and dangerous. No one sees them enter the swirling mists and no one is there when only one man emerges to begin his descent. Back in civilisation, the lone climber says that his companion fell to his death. But did he slip or was he pushed? Who is to say? And that was roughly the scenario at the heart of the mystery of the Arran Murderer.

In July 1889, in the heyday of holidays down the coast to the Firth of Clyde resorts from Glasgow, a young London clerk called Edwin Rose boarded a steamer heading from Rothesay to the island of Arran on holiday. On board he met Laurie, then twenty-five, and they chummed up with another couple of young passengers. Laurie and Rose shared the same lodgings on the island and with the others went on boating and walking trips to sample the delights of the island that is known as "Scotland in miniature" since it has all the attributes of the beautiful mountainous West coast and some areas that resemble good Lowland farming land – all in one reasonably-sized island.

One of the main attractions of the place was, and still is, the mountain known as Goatfell. Laurie wanted Rose to go climbing on it with him. Oddly one of the other young men – who were at the end of their holiday and going home the next day – warned Rose not to go. But the warning was ignored. Laurie and Rose left their lodgings without saying where they were going and the landlady suspected they were doing a "runner" to avoid paying their bill. Rose never made it back home, and not long after, Rose's brother arrived on the island and could not find him anywhere. A search was started involving around 200 people, a massive exercise in such a place. Rose was eventually found under a bush, or some say, stuffed into a stone crypt. He appeared to have been beaten to death with stones. After the discovery of the body a shepherd came forward to say he had seen Laurie coming off the hill alone, looking tired out. And Laurie had also been seen leaving the island by steamer.

Back on the mainland Laurie moved about a lot and after a while settled in Liverpool, where he dismissed with a laugh stories that he was about to be arrested and charged with a murder in faraway Arran. But he returned to Scotland and was spotted on a train by a policeman and chased to a wood where he made a half-hearted attempt to cut his own throat. Taken to Edinburgh for trial he admitted in court to robbing Rose but denied killing him, claiming his companion had fallen to his death. The story was that he had simply robbed his new friend and hidden the body and fled. Laurie was sentenced to hang but was reprieved and given a life sentence. He could have been sent to a hospital for the criminally insane but was instead sent to Peterhead, where he was a difficult prisoner and like many another convict before him, he endlessly claimed to anyone who would listen that he was innocent of the killing, if not the theft, from Rose.

As we have seen earlier, conditions in the jail at that time were horrendous but nonetheless the victim's brother declaimed in letters to the press that Laurie had got off lightly. He would have much preferred the Glasgow man to swing – which might have been a real miscarriage of justice. No blood was found on Laurie's clothes and there was medical evidence that a fall could have killed Rose. The evidence was mainly circumstantial but he still had to listen to a judge in a black cap initially pronounce his doom.

In reporting the sensational trial of Laurie, the *Scotsman* said: "It was held with every manifestation of public interest." Queues formed each day to hear at first-hand the gruesome nature of the crime. The public fury at Laurie was fuelled by the revelation that on the evening of the death of Rose he was seen drinking in the Corrie Bar, and later he carried around a striped blazer belonging to Rose.

But if it had been carefully planned crime rather than an opportunistic theft Laurie was remarkably careless, leaving several obvious clues that showed he had been beside the body. And other climbers had seen them at the summit of Goatfell. What really happened will never be known. But that trip north to Peterhead got Laurie a place in the jail's history. He was one of the first men to escape from it.

The story was told in the local press under the, to these days, tame headline: EXCITING INCIDENT AT PETERHEAD PRISON – THE ESCAPE AND CAPTURE OF LAURIE. Not quite how *The Sun* or the *Daily Record* would put it today. But the story was, as one news editor of mine liked to say, a belter. The first escaper had been an Aberdeenshire burglar, much lower down the pecking order of infamy than Laurie. This hapless fellow had barely gone half a mile when he stumbled into the arms of a policeman. However, the paper noted that on this occasion, "fleet of foot as he was", Laurie never got out of sight of the prison either.

By the time of his escape he had been in the prison for a couple of years or so and despite being difficult early in his term he had been of such good behaviour latterly that he had become a prisoner of the "first class" and had privileges not given to the normal con. He was said to be of surly disposition and a regular in making groundless complaints about conditions in the prison but he was a first-class workman entrusted with valuable tasks in the carpenters' shop. This facilitated his escape, as he was in a gang erecting scaffolding used during work on warders' houses when he made a break for freedom. It seemed the perfect opportunity on a foggy morning to leap over some of the planking used in the scaffolding and leg it away from the prison.

Once over the wall, however, there was no real cover for an escaper to hide in the days before the prison was surrounded by houses, and despite crossing a hayfield and leaping over a few dry stane dykes, one of the prison civil guards caught him almost immediately. Not much of an escape compared to the feats of those who later managed to get out of cells and over the walls and stay on the run for days at a time, but an escape nonetheless. Back in the prison his mental condition was reassessed and he was sent to Perth Criminal Asylum for the Insane and he died in 1930.

Laurie had originally arrived in Peterhead after some months of probation in Perth prison immediately after his trial and when he was taken north his status as a "lifer" was marked with a black crêpe band on his arm. A newspaper of the day wrote about his life in jail after escaping the noose. Despite the somewhat archaic language, this was a feature that would have graced any tabloid today. The writer answered the questions about the Arran Murderer's life in jail. It was said that his work in the prison was not hard but irksome – teasing piles of hessian into oakum, tarred fibres used in wooden ships. On his arrival in Peterhead in 1890 he wore Perth prison clothes: "a moleskin jacket and vest and a stock of the same for the neck, stamped all over with broad arrows." He was also provided with a moleskin bonnet with his prison number on it. His underclothes were said to be a "pair of drawers, cotton or plaiding, the latter in winter." His shirt was of unbleached cotton in summer and plaiding in winter. The uniform in Peterhead was similar though a coat was provided and a red shirt.

The diet in Perth was described in some detail and it was said that in Peterhead the food was slightly better. For breakfast in Perth there was 8oz of oatmeal made into porridge and three-fourths of a pint of milk. For dinner there was two pints of barley broth, which "is made of ox heads and haugh, suet and vegetables," and three-fourths of a pound of wheaten bread. Supper was 2lb of potatoes, or porridge in lieu. The Peterhead *table d'hote* was similar except with – not surprisingly considering the location – an occasional helping of fresh fish.

Entertainment there was none. A twenty-minute visit every four months was allowed and receiving and sending a letter again every four months was permitted. It was a very hard regime.

The newspaper went on to inform its curious readers that the convicts worked in the quarry or the breakwater and that they were supervised by warders and backed up by civil guards with carbines. These officers were said to "take up a position of advantage covering the convicts." Escape or mutiny seemed unlikely, especially since the cons worked wearing leg irons with several pounds of lead attached to their feet. This was described with considerable under-statement as a "safeguard" against trouble. In a further horrifying description of the convict's life in the nineteenth century, the writer went on to explain that if for weather or other reasons the cons could not work as normal in the quar-ries or breakwaters they were put on some sort of machine called "the crash" which had to be manually turned 14,500 times a day every day except Saturday when it was reduced to 10,000 turns. There were no hi-tech gyms around these days but no doubt "the crash" would keep the cons in good physical shape. The author also mentioned one other nice little touch in the prison regime – once you had served the appropriate time the moleskins could be replaced by serge.

About the same time of the Laurie escape incident it is

interesting, if not surprising, to note that the punishing conditions in the jail were becoming too much for some of the convicts. Any real chance of escape was negligible and years of misery stretched ahead for most of the cons who were on long sentences, and many a mile from their homes and relatives. No TV in cells, no snooker leagues, no gym, no recreation and seriously bad food in a difficult climate. Little wonder thoughts turned to suicide. Even that was difficult, with the guards constantly watching their charges.

One man in 1893 was so desperate to end it all that he took the almost unthinkable way out of drinking red lead paint when working in the prison yard. He had been sent back into the jail on an errand for a warder and on his return he spotted a pot of the paint lying handy. Before his keepers could stop him, he grabbed it and swallowed around a quart of the fluid before the poison was snatched from him. Medical help was immediately given and a report on the incident made a point that is not too difficult to understand or to be horrified that "the large quantity of poisonous matter taken greatly helped to effect its own cure." It would certainly have been difficult to keep such an unpleasant substance down. The desperate man survived in the prison hospital in a "weak but not dangerous" condition.

The day before this drama there had been some excitement at the quarry at Stirling Hill, where a work party had been taken on the little private train from the prison. There does not seem to have been much trouble down the years on the train itself, probably because the passengers were tightly herded into the compartments and closely watched by the guards. But out in the quarry it was a different matter, as the gangs of men were able to roam around the site getting on with their work. There was more opportunity for a sudden attack here. On this occasion a convict had leapt at a guard when he was distracted and tried to "throttle" him. But the prison staff were not pushovers and the attacked officer was able to push off his assailant and then whack him so hard with his baton that he broke his arm. The con was taken to the prison hospital, a busy place at times, and his arm was set. His impulsive reckless act earned him some more prison time. This was just one attack of many on the warders at this time. Desperate men would resort to desperate actions.

The quarry at this time was a dangerous place in other ways, as the death of convict Henry Hanley, a twenty-five-year-old Glaswegian, demonstrates. It took a fatal accident inquiry to show that at least Major Dodd, the first governor, who was ultimately in charge of the safety, was not allowing extra risks to be taken in the Admiralty quarry just because the labourers were convicted criminals. Hanley lost his life in an accident that could equally have happened in a civilian quarry. The procedures the accident inquiry found were much as those used in commercial quarries. The *modus operandi* was that experienced civilian foremen and shot firers worked with the cons. The quarry staff did not direct the cons themselves but got the warders to pass on instruction, but that did not cause the accident. Blasting the night before had left a twelve-ton lump of rock perched on the side of a steep slope. Attempts to move it with a "seam" shot placed by the expert shot firer had failed. Smaller stones wedged under the boulder were preventing it moving. To resolve the problem these stones needed to be removed.

Hanley and another con called Murray were set to the task. The young Glaswegian had a rope round his waist so that he could be pulled to safety by his colleagues if anything went wrong. At least, that was the idea. The stone moved and an attempt to haul Hanley to safety by the men holding the rope ends was made. However, the rope slipped up from Hanley's waist to his chest and he was left dangling over a fifty-foot drop. Murray was luckier and witnesses told of seeing him leaping to safety from rock to rock as the huge boulder thundered down on him.

There was much wrangling at the inquiry about the type of knot used on Hanley's rope. Some said it was a running knot, others a sailor's knot. No matter, it ended up "round the victim's chest and a medical examination showed that his breast bone was broken in three places. The second, third and fourth ribs on the right side were broken into fragments and the left leg broken in several places." This it was said, in a matter-of-fact fashion, would have been enough to kill Hanley. It was a painful death. A single crushing blow from that twelve-ton boulder might have been a kinder fate than to be left dangling on a rope in bizarre fashion high over the quarry with the life being squeezed out of him agonisingly minute by minute. But at least the inquiry made clear that the death of the convict could have happened in the same way to any quarry worker in "any part of the kingdom." Not much consolation though to Hanley or his relatives.

4

A POLITICAL PRISONER, HUNGER STRIKES AND WAR ON WAR

Peterhead has from time to time been called "Scotland's gulag," though to most of its inmates down the years, who had little interest in or knowledge of politics, such a description may be a tad on the esoteric side. The concerns of those removed from society and held for long years in that cold, hard fortress, seldom deviated from a desire to be free again to knife a gangland rival or rob a bank or two. They were not revolutionaries, just conscienceless criminals on the hunt for cash or bent on settling old gangland or personal scores. But, as always, there was an exception or two. Some of the Red Clydesiders served time in Barlinnie and Peterhead. These pioneer socialists had an altogether different set of concerns from the majority of the prisoners: they wanted to improve the lives of their fellow men.

Workers' leaders in the early part of the last century faced the constant threat of arrest and trial. It might not have been Russia or Germany, but the knock on the door by a uniformed policeman was a daily fear for such as Tom Bell, John Wheatley, John Muir, John Maxton, Willie

Gallacher and John Maclean. John Maclean in particular was dealt with extremely harshly by the authorities, who were angered by his passionate and constant campaigning against the slaughter of the First World War. In Glasgow he held hugely well-attended rallies in Bath Street and on his Southside patch in Shawlands. A true legend in his lifetime he had a large army of followers, pacifists and anti-war protesters. At one time they held regular meetings in the old Metropole Theatre (later the home of the Logans, the legendary show business dynasty) in Stockwell Street in the city centre on Sunday nights. In the early days of the First World War with young patriots dying in their thousands in the fight against Germany, it took courage to speak out publicly against the war. But Maclean did not lack guts. He proclaimed: "I have been enlisted in the socialist army for fifteen years. God damn all other armies. Any soldier who shoots another soldier in the war is a murderer." This powerful and controversial public speaking on the morality of war was deemed by the authorities as likely to harm the war effort and prejudice recruiting.

It was not a problem exclusive to Scotland or the Scots. An anarchist and revolutionary called Guy Aldred, who despite being a Londoner had settled in Glasgow, was, like Maclean, arrested for his views and jailed, though he did not end up in Peterhead. In August 1916 he was ordered to be detained after an appearance at Winchester and sent to a work camp in Dyce near Aberdeen, just thirty odd miles south of Peterhead. This was almost a worse fate than spending time in one of Scotland's regular prisons. The prisoners were held in a tented village in primitive conditions, barely surviving in a sea of mud. They were put to work on hard labour in a local quarry just like the Peterhead cons. But unlike a real

39

prison, escape from such tented prisons was relatively easy and Aldred was among those who did a "runner," though he was recaptured in a relatively short time and this time sent to a conventional jail in the south. There his agitation – he was ringleader in a prisoners' strike – got him what was called "number one punishment," a bland way of describing forty-two days in solitary with three days on bread and water and three without food, locked in a bare and unheated cell.

There were several other such work camps in Britain, their existence obscured by government secrecy that constrained the newspaper coverage of the war. Astonishingly, sixty-nine conscientious objectors died in these places that were little more than the British equivalent of the work camps of the enemy. It is interesting that writers looking at the history of the Dyce camp record that the inmates were given respect and, on some occasions, help by the locals. Perhaps the prisoners' rebellious attitudes struck a chord with the infamously "thrawn" North-Easterners who rarely like to swim with the tide. Maybe, too, it says something about the relationship between the local folk and Peterhead jail itself, which was highlighted by the support that escapers like Gentle Johnny Ramensky generated. The story of such camps as the one at Dyce is a largely forgotten but important part of the penal history of these isles.

Early arrests of Maclean had been made under the catch-all of breach of the peace charges, which were brought after his well-attended anti-war meetings in the city of Glasgow. Now the more powerful Defence of the Realm Act was sending him to jail. At one stage the firebrand found himself held in Edinburgh Castle as a "prisoner of war" and given the choice of a court martial or appearing in the civil High

Court. On this occasion he opted for his day in court but was rewarded with a three-year jail sentence. It is interesting that his fellow citizens of Glasgow, despite their general patriotism and support of the boys dying in the trenches, could muster a huge rally of 100,000 in Glasgow Green to demand his release. The good folk of the city recognised his socialist sincerity and passionately-held beliefs. Even if they disagreed with him. He was a truly remarkable man, but in Peterhead he found himself surrounded by common criminals rather than political agitators and intellectuals. Hunger strikes were a regular weapon for such caged dissidents as himself and he damaged his health in prison and endured the disgusting procedure of force-feeding.

Maclean is still, long after his death in 1923, a revered figure in British left-wing politics. His legacy spawned many books, poems and songs. Hugh MacDiarmid wrote: "Of all Maclean's foes not one was his peer." And in another poem he described him as "both beautiful and red." No wonder Maclean is still being written about in the age of the World Wide Web and socialists in many countries still delve into his story. In a Scottish Republican Socialist Movement document there is a remarkable picture of life in Peterhead which first appeared in the publication *The Red Dawn* in March 1919. This account of his time in the North-East was rediscovered by Jim Clayton, the author of *John MacLean and the Conspiracies*.

Maclean's own story of his experiences "up north," as the Glasgow cons say, is fascinating. He contrasted life in what he called a Glasgow "local" prison, Duke Street, with the daily "scientific torture" of what he rather oddly described in a piece of tautology "a convict prison." He told his readers how your hair is cropped short and cut once a fortnight to

41

keep it that way. However, a thick knitted cap was provided and it "kept the head quite warm." Hygiene was rather different in those far-off days and it will come as a surprise to today's readers that underclothing was kept "clean and sanitary" by being washed once a fortnight! The political prisoner felt that the inadequate clothing supplied to those working outside the prison in quarries or at the harbour was an official ploy to damage their health by causing colds, flu and other illnesses. His cell was of the regular dimensions of the time – about four-feet broad, eight-feet long and seven-feet high. But in 1918 two cells were knocked together for English prisoners brought north, though why they should get special privileges is not clear. The authorities were obviously still keen on the idea of prisoners using their time to good effect and the English cons were there to construct a little aerodrome near Peterhead harbour.

Maclean described how the glass in his cell was twisted so badly that little light entered the tiny space and you could not see out at all. The idea he wrote, perhaps with a touch of paranoia, was to make prisoners brood and fret, and he highlighted the Sunday misery of fellow prisoners who could not even read to help pass the time on the day of rest. The heating system was primitive and inadequate and furthermore the prisoners were not allowed, by decree of the governor, to wrap their blankets round themselves when not in bed. Strange that even that little kindness was denied to those serving time in such a miserable place.

The daily routine was horrendous. A bell was rung at 5am and prisoners had to get up and wash and make their beds until about 5.30, when orderlies served porridge and skimmed milk. At 7 the cell doors were opened and prisoners headed out, guarded by warders, to the yard in designated groups and then proceeded "to work, formerly in the quarry, but latterly to the Admiralty yard." Before leaving the prison they were searched. At 11.30 the prisoners were re-formed into parties and searched again before "dinner," which was broth, beef, bread and potatoes, or sometimes cheese. It was back to work from 1pm till 5.30 and then back to the prison where 14oz of dry bread and a pint of coffee was given out. Prisoners were then free to read if they could or otherwise entertain themselves until 8.30pm.

Maclean, an avid reader, noted that the books provided were selected to exclude anything to do with murder, suicide and other morbid ideas which were not healthy. This is not the case these days when prison libraries give access to the full range of the world of literature – and in some cases even DVDs of crime films, though that raises the blood pressure of the folk who think a life behind bars is overly cushy.

The quality of thought of the great socialist and a certain fair-mindedness on his part is evident in his writings at this time. His confinement ended in forced feeding and other tortures, including he claimed, drugging his food, but he could still remark that the provision of clothing, regular food, a dry bed and relatively short hours of labour was still a better life than that endured by the poor outside of the prison walls. Which is a remarkable insight into the way life was lived all these years ago.

Some of the warders, too, showed a humanitarian side and an order that prisoners were not supposed to speak to each other except in connection with their work was largely ignored. If you discounted the "scientific torture" he wrote about, he wryly remarked that twenty years in Peterhead might be better than ten years down a mine in the days when mine owners exploited their workers and thought little of their lives. In prison your "employers" did not take risks with your life to line their pockets. But it was no place for an educated and idealistic man driven by a passion to improve life for his fellows.

Maclean died young and Peterhead played a role, his physical health torn from him by the savage conditions in jail. Books, however, saved his mental health and he left a considerable legacy of socialist thinking. And one thing is for sure: John Maclean was certainly not your run-of-the-mill Peterhead con.

5

JUSTICE FOR THE CAGED INNOCENTS

Those who believe that only the guilty go to jail, the sort of folk – and there are still some around today – who insist that "they wouldna be in the dock if they hadna done it" should take a look at the evidence and the statistics. Those who confidently proclaim that the English and Scottish systems of law and judgement are the finest in the world might be, in the totality of things, correct. But they are in a dream-world if they also believe that there are no innocents in jail or indeed that no innocent man ended his days dangling at the end of a rope. I remember going round Barlinnie with a recent governor, Bill McKinley, a much respected high flier in the prison service, now retired, and as we spoke to a group of inmates he remarked, "Any innocent men in here?" Many a hand shot into the air. And everyone, prisoners and visitor alike, had a quiet smile. But there was a chance that this straw poll in a jail holding some of the toughest residents of Glasgow, a city known worldwide for having a high proportion of hard men with no respect for the law, was probably not completely wrong.

Of course, you can't always be sure. Cases of wrongful

imprisonment come to light with remarkable regularity. But in this case, in Barlinnie, any con fitted up by the police or otherwise wrongly imprisoned would likely be someone with a record as long as your arm who on release would soon return, this time genuinely guilty. Such claims of innocence are a prison commonplace. I was even told by a long-term Peterhead prisoner, Walter Norval, who features elsewhere in this book, that one day a fellow convict remarked over a mug of tea, in matter-of-fact fashion, that he had not committed the offence for which he was serving time. Walter thought that if this was the case his friend should fight as hard as possible to be cleared and released. But this con was having none of it – he was prepared to do the time even if in this case he had not done the crime. He pointed out without rancour that he had escaped punishment for many a crime he HAD committed and that if he pushed the case too far the real culprit, a friend, would be arrested. This guy reasoned that he should have been in the jail anyway!

But all this minor stuff is a far cry from major miscarriages of justice that flaw the British record. Some years ago I was sent a remarkable book by Thomas Toughill that claimed to have solved the mystery of the Oscar Slater case. It had a fascinating foreword by Peter Hill, who originated in BBC TV's *Rough Justice* programme in the late 1970s. Peterhead prison is prominent in the history of wrongful imprisonment – four of its most infamous and best-known inmates spent long years in it for crimes they did not commit – Oscar Slater, Paddy Meehan and TC Campbell and Joe Steele of the Glasgow Ice Cream War miscarriage. Maybe too the Arran Murderer Laurie, who may have been innocent. But Hill puts all that in perspective with the facts of some English wrongful imprisonments of which, as you might expect of a

46

more populous country, there are many more. Mostly they hinge on mistaken identity, which was a major factor in the Slater and Meehan cases as well, and Hill provides some striking examples.

Adolf Beck is a name often linked with that of Slater as classic examples of witnesses mistaking identities. Beck was convicted in England for crimes committed by a George Smith, and despite Beck's protestation that he was in the clear, a jury swallowed flawed evidence and he was convicted. But it later emerged that Smith had been circumcised but Beck hadn't, a discovery that crushed the evidence and clearly indicated mistaken identity. This led to the conviction being overturned. At that time England had no procedure for releasing the innocent Beck, which in turn led to the creation of the English Court of Appeal. This was back in 1907. Similarly, years later, the Slater case had a role in the creation of the Scottish Court of Criminal Appeal. Oscar Slater served eighteen years in Peterhead – as convict no.1992 – breaking rocks in the prison quarry before being released but not officially cleared of the murder of Marion Gilchrist.

The crime that had landed Slater long years of hell was not your usual low-life Glasgow murder. Nor was he a typical Glasgow criminal. It took place a few days before Christmas of 1908 in fashionable West Princes Street in the west end of the city. This was home to many of the most prosperous folk of Scotland's industrial capital who lived in some style, in dramatic contrast to those who lived and worked in the less salubrious east end. As the holiday approached the dull gas-lit streets were brightened a little by a few Christmas wreaths and decorations, and the brass knockers and letter-boxes on the solid wood doors had an extra shine. Even the

47

usually gloomy Glasgow weather could not dispel a sense of expectation of the Christmas and New Year celebrations, particularly the New Year, which in Scotland at the time was the more important of the two winter festivals. Miss Gilchrist fitted the area well, expensively dressed and well-connected – the newspapers of the time called her "rich," adding an extra dimension to her killing. She was found battered to death not long after sending her maid out to buy a newspaper. The servant returned to find a neighbour at her mistress's door who said he had been alerted by a loud thud just moments before. Suddenly, as they talked, a smartly-dressed stranger brushed past them rushing to the head of the stairs and legging it for the street, clearly determined to put as much distance between him and the flat as quickly as possible.

The maid and the neighbour then went into the dining room of the house, where they found Miss Gilchrist lying battered and badly injured. She died a short time later without giving any clue who her murderous assailant had been. The only thing that seemed to be missing was a gold and diamond brooch.

It was on the face of it a simple scenario: an opportunist robbery by some local rascal. But the way the story played out is in hindsight remarkable in several ways. First is the fact that Oscar Slater was to be fitted up as the killer by the establishment. It is astonishing to anyone looking at the case now to believe that he was involved at all and over the years evidence has emerged to confirm that almost certainly he did not even know who Marion Gilchrist was, and with complete certainty, it can be said he was not the man who ran down the stairs past her maid.

It was a high-profile case featured heavily in the press

and, as happens to this day, the police were put under pressure to find a murderer who had caused a sensation in a douce part of the city where crime was not commonplace. It is the old story of the media and public opinion screeching that "something must be done" and desperate and clueless investigators clutching at any straw or hint to come out of the underworld. Such pressure on the police has caused hundreds of wrongful convictions.

The first urge is, of course, to turn to the usual suspects. But Slater was no master criminal with a long record of violence and well known to the cops. If a criminal at all, he was definitely small-time. He only came to the attention of the investigators when they were tipped off anonymously that he had tried to sell a pawn ticket for a brooch.

Now he was in their sights, the police enthusiastically probed the background of the supposed seller of the pawn ticket. Slater did not come up sparkling white under scrutiny. In fact, it would have pleased many a Glasgow citizen if he had genuinely been the killer, as it would have confirmed their prejudices. There was a lot of anti-German feeling in the city at the time and he was a German Jew with a sleazy reputation. He lived with a glamorous mistress with show business connections; he was a gambler and a jewel dealer. If anyone was looking for someone to stitch up he was, on paper, the ideal candidate. He was put into the frame, as they say, despite the fact that it was easy to prove that the jewellery sold by him had no connection with old Miss Gilchrist. This little inconvenience did not seem to deter the police one little bit – desperation to prove a theory was paramount. Or maybe there was a more sinister explanation. Do not let the facts spoil a good theory, as some journalists say.

The suspicion now is that Oscar Slater was becoming the perfect patsy in the hunt for the murderer. An ideal man for their purposes had fallen into the lap of those in high places who wanted to protect the real killer. Slater was demonised in the papers and became a hate figure to the public, who read with enthusiasm verging on voyeurism about his sleazy background. To most who followed the case the revelations of mistresses and gambling were an insight into a side of Glasgow they had never seen.

Slater did nothing to help his own case by inexplicably travelling at short notice with his mistress to New York, where he was arrested. He then returned to Scotland of his own free will, confident that no police force in the world could convict him since, apart from anything else, he had an alibi. And he had no connection with the missing brooch. It was a big mistake. An identification parade was held with witnesses who later claimed to have been prompted by the police to finger him. The trial was a farce with no solid evidence to convict him other than that dodgy ID parade. But as a hated foreigner in a strange city he was convicted both by the real court and the court of public opinion.

The identification point is interesting because for almost a hundred years this case has been pored over by criminologists and there was some evidence in their findings that Slater had a slight resemblance to one of Miss Gilchrist's relatives. This gives credence to the theory that a family member was involved in the killing, if not the actual murderer, and that the motive was a dispute over money or a will and the stealing of the brooch a red herring.

The Gilchrist family had close contact with high society and with the top legal elite in Scotland at the time. In takes no great leap of imagination to suppose that they could be involved in a plot to frame Slater. He was granted mercy just hours before he was due to die on the gallows at Glasgow's old Duke Street prison. That decision itself is very suspicious, giving credence to the idea that the authorities were not too worried about such a character as Oscar Slater being sentenced to years of misery in the Peterhead stone quarries but drew the line at killing an innocent man. Whatever, speculation continues even today and Thomas Toughill's *Oscar Slater – the Mystery Solved* (Canongate, Edinburgh, 1993) is a must read however for anyone wanting a meticulous and lengthy examination of all the theories in detail.

So, instead of a sudden drop into eternity Slater was transported north to Peterhead, where he began a hard new career smashing stone in all kinds of weather, playing a part in the creation of Peterhead's Harbour of Refuge. It was a life much different from the tiled closes and stained glass of the beautiful west end tenements and the gambling saloons and loose women of Glasgow at the turn of the last century. And Oscar Slater was not the perfect prisoner. The ache of his wrongful incarceration ate at him night and day. He constantly proclaimed his innocence, as you would do, and he showed at all times how he resented his treatment. It is said that in the prison he was on occasion involved in fights, though violence played no role in his earlier life. If he had hopes that his sentence would be reviewed after fifteen years, as sometimes happened, he was to be disappointed. The anti-German feeling after the First World War did not help but, in any case, to the public he was a largely forgotten figure.

Arthur Conan Doyle, though, was a supporter. The great writer of detective stories and, it has to be said, the man behind some eccentric flawed investigations of spiritualist phenomena, had a reputation for fighting against injustice and knew the Slater case well. He studied it for years and from the start he was clear in his mind that it was a fit-up. His concerns about the injustice of the case were shared by others at the top in journalism, the famous criminologist of the time, Thomas Roughead, and some of the police officers involved, especially a Lieutenant Trench, who was himself unjustly treated by his superiors for supporting the theories of Slater's innocence.

The years of clamour created by Slater's supporters resulted in the German eventually being freed from Peterhead on a technicality in 1928. But even then the authorities would not go the last mile and admit he had been framed all these years ago and he was never officially cleared of the murder. But at least the mean-minded elite had let him out of prison. On release he lived quietly in Glasgow and Ayr. Surprisingly, he was seemingly happy to stay in the country where the authorities had conspired to send him, an innocent man, to the verge of death on the gallows. Few who knew him are still with us, but one elderly man I spoke to recently, in the course of research for this book, remembered as a youngster living up the same genteel tenement close as him in Glasgow's Shawlands. Slater, whose name will forever be linked with Peterhead, was an unlikely ex-con to his neighbours – on leaving his flat in immaculate dress he would descend the stairs on his way to the streets and whatever business he had that day. But if he passed a youngster on the way down he would stop and benignly hand him or her a wee sweetie. A far cry from prison porridge in the North-East of Scotland.

Oscar Slater was not the only innocent who lodged for years in Peterhead. The case of Paddy Meehan, the man wrongly convicted in 1969 of the murder of pensioner Rachel Ross in, coincidentally, Slater's adopted hometown of Ayr, has many similarities to that of the German, including a celebrity supporter. In Meehan's case, instead of Conan Doyle, TV personality and author Ludovic Kennedy led the fight to free him, supported by a group of newspaper men and lawyers. Meehan, like Slater, was involved in a possibly rigged identity parade and there were accusations of evidence being planted on him to help ensure a conviction. Even the furore in the press was similar to that which followed the death of old Marion Gilchrist. History does indeed seem to repeat itself.

The victim in the Meehan case, Rachel Ross, was a seventy-two-year-old who lived with her ex-bookmaker husband in a bungalow in the Clyde coast resort of Ayr. They were involved in bingo halls and kept large sums of money in the house, something that seemed to be known in the murky Glasgow underworld. Their home was a tempting target for any rascal bent on getting his hands on large sums of readies and the brutal murder horrified the entire country. Intruders had broken into the home of the wealthy couple and tied them up. Mrs Ross was bludgeoned heavily around the head and later died in hospital. The couple were not found in the house until twenty-four hours after the thieves had left. The detail of their ordeal made horrific reading in the press and, once again, the police found themselves under enormous public pressure to find the cruel villains involved.

Again not for the first time, in an investigation without any obvious leads, they pulled in one of the usual suspects in break-ins, Paddy Meehan. This despite the fact they were dealing with a violent incident and that Meehan, although a well-known safebreaker and burglar, was not considered a man of violence.

Meehan had been suspected of being in the area on the night of the crime. He was, but he was returning to Glasgow with a co-villain Jim Griffiths after some nefarious late-night business south of Ayr. Griffiths did have a record of violence and a pathological fear of imprisonment. Approached by the police about his movements on the night of the murder he went berserk and went on a daylight rampage through the streets of Glasgow. By the time he was cornered and killed by a shot from armed police who had chased him into a tenement flat in the west end, nine men had been shot by him, one fatally, plus two women, a child and a police officer. The officer who killed him had, as per police practice, aimed at his shoulder but the bullet ricocheted into his heart.

Griffiths, aged thirty-four, was buried in an unmarked pauper's grave in Linn Park cemetery in Glasgow's south-side. His life had run its course, but for Meehan the nightmare was only beginning. The saga of his wrongful conviction and eventual pardon made headlines for years and is told in detail in my book *Glasgow's Hard Men* (Black & White Publishing, Edinburgh, 2002). One major difference in the Slater and Meehan cases is that in the Ayr murder the killer was found. It was established many years later that the real murderer was an infamous Glasgow low-lifer called Tank McGuiness, who eventually died in a bloody street brawl. No matter, in the late 1960s, after a dramatic and controversial trial, Paddy Meehan took that road so familiar to Glasgow's criminals up north to Peterhead. In jail he was soon a headache to staff and governor alike. As Slater had done before him, he took every opportunity to declaim his innocence and show the size of the gigantic chip on his shoulder. Again, like in the Slater case, the outsider thinking of a man wrongly banged up in a tough jail and enduring a tough regime could sympathise. There can be no harder torture to endure than years of imprisonment for a crime you did not commit. Especially as no one inside the prison would listen to you.

Meehan refused to take any part in prison chores or cooperate with the prison authorities – in a reversal of the old prison cliché, he was doing the time but had not done the crime, and it showed in his behaviour. You suspect such a demonstration of his feelings consistently over the years must have aroused some sympathy from some of his jailors but there is not much sign of it. It was those on the outside who listened to his pleas of innocence and decided to do something about it. Those in the prison service can be good judges of character and you wonder how many believed that this small-time Glasgow crook was capable of such a wickedly cruel murder as that of Mrs Ross. But even if some had a sneaking sympathy for him and an unexpressed belief in his claims to be innocent, it made little difference to Paddy's life in jail. His constant hassle with the prison rulebook and the harder of his tormentors meant there was only one solution to get everyone a little peace – sling him into solitary. The astonishing fact is that this punishment was not for a weekend or two to teach a difficult prisoner a lesson. In his time in Peterhead Paddy Meehan spent seven years in solitary confinement. In the annals of crime this must be among the most draconian punishment handed out to an innocent man. Other than to be left dangling at the end of rope in the Barlinnie hanging shed.

Meehan was eventually pardoned in 1976, but unlike

Slater who lived life after Peterhead out of the limelight, Paddy sought out the late-night company of Glasgow's often drouthy newsmen and was a familiar figure in the city's pubs. He even used his old skills in burglary as a security advisor. But after he left jail Paddy was most prominent for the years he spent in conflict with the authorities over his compensation and in a feud with legendary lawyer Joe Beltrami. This was a bit unsettling for Joe, who had played a major role in the campaign to free him. Meehan postulated all sorts of wild theories on how he had come to end up in prison, including accusations that the British Secret Service was to blame. He even wrote a book which included this fantasy, and many a Glaswegian remembers seeing him as a tragic figure trying to hawk this slim volume on the streets of the city for ready cash. The city booksellers had refused to handle it, wary of the legal implications of the content. He died of throat cancer in 1994 aged sixty-seven.

Slater and Meehan were only two of the better-known difficult prisoners of Peterhead. Down the years a succession of toerags made life difficult for the men in the north who had joined the prison service, often for job security in an area where that could be hard to find. From day one there were troublemakers, there always are. In any hard prison fighting the regime is fruitless 99.9 per cent of the time, but you will always get those who try. Even those whose chance of getting anyone to listen to their protestations of innocence, never mind getting a celebrity campaign to back their claims, is as likely as a big win on the lottery. But someone like TC Campbell is rather different. No one with the slightest interest in matters criminal in this country is unaware of perhaps the most modern injustice linked with Peterhead – Glasgow's infamous Ice Cream War murders.

Campbell and another Glasgow hard man, Joe Steele, were wrongly convicted of these dreadful killings. Campbell in particular was aware that his constant wars with the Peterhead rulers made headlines in the Glasgow papers for years and kept the injustice he had suffered in the mind of the general public. He and Steele were as driven as Slater and Meehan when they languished behind the very same bars.

Steele had an interesting history coming from a notorious Glasgow crime family (a genuine family, not in the mafia way!). His brother John, known in his frequent visits to Scotland's prisons as "Johnnyboy," was a headache when in Peterhead, being involved in the infamous dirty protests, the stories of which made regular headlines and outraged the readers of the tabloids. These protests were a feature of life in the jail for many years around the 1970s and '80s. Cons with a chip on their shoulder about beatings and horrific treatment from the bad apples among the prison officers took to smearing the walls of their cells with excrement and urinated everywhere and anywhere. Dirty was something of an understatement. It is difficult to properly state the effect this nastiest form of protest had on the majority of arrow-straight warders who were only trying to do a job. What shocking memories these men took home with them at the end of a shift. Johnnyboy and Jimmy Boyle were two of the well-known criminals involved.

The Steele clan were just one of many criminal families in Glasgow. Evil thickened the blood of many a law-breaking dynasty – the Ferris, Thompson and Steele families prominent among them. One prison governor told me of having a grandfather, father and grandson of one bunch all in his nick at one time or another. John Steele was also a bit of a jail breaker, though not in the class of Johnny Ramensky when it came to the Houdini stuff.

Johnnyboy was also something of an amateur psychologist, with himself as the subject. In a book he wrote about his life of crime he dwelt heavily on a childhood of beatings from his father and the horrors of deprivation in a tough Glasgow scheme. One of the deprivations was psychological – the absence of a law-abiding role model. Like many another Glaswegian he had relatives galore who feared the cops and knew the jails of the country like the backs of their hands. When he finally ended up in Peterhead prison, life came as no surprise to him; he had listened to jail tales galore at the family fireside.

No crime in recent years has so horrified the Scottish public as that of the deaths of the Doyle family in their Bankend Street, Glasgow, home as result of a deliberate act of arson. James Doyle Snr, fifty-three; James Doyle Jnr, twenty-three; Tony Doyle, fourteen; Andrew Doyle, eighteen; their sister Christine Halleron, twenty-five; and baby Mark Halleron, aged one, all died when their flat was set alight. The deaths of the Doyles was a result of various gang feuds over the control of the many profitable ice cream vans that patrolled the mean streets of the Glasgow schemes. The honest traders were being attacked and driven out by ruthless gang lords who realised there was more money to be made by such vans than that generated by flogging mere confectionary. The sales of ice cream, lollipops and cigarettes was becoming a front for the distribution of hard drugs much in demand in these deprived areas. In the weeks and months before the fiery death of the Doyles, who had a son in the ice cream van trade, the city police were kept busy investigating attacks, and the threat of attacks, on the honest traders. The Bankend Street massacre was the final push to convince decent folk in the ice cream business to hand over vans to the neds who would promptly turn them into mobile illegal drug dispensaries. No prescription needed, just hard cash. And the best of "gear."

When news of the deadly blaze first broke in 1984, the newspapers treated it as a not unusual Friday night fire. It made the splash in the Saturday morning front page of the *Evening Times* but there was no early hint of the real story behind the tragedy – that it was arson. Glasgow had the nickname "tinder box city" and to the veterans on the Saturday morning news desks the fire at first seemed pretty run-of-the-mill. But this was no drunken chip pan incident, nor was it caused by that other Glasgow serial failing, careless use of candles in a dangerous effort to cut the electricity bill. As the death toll mounted as the victims slowly succumbed to their horrific burns it became clear that this tragedy was gang driven and the story grew to dominate the front pages for weeks. Yet again the police were under the cosh of public opinion and yet again the usual suspects were looked at.

Campbell and Steele were no Sunday school teachers, they were major players in the Glasgow crime scene feared by the folk who had them living in their midst and constantly at odds with the forces of law and order. They were pulled in. Their pleas of innocence were ignored and they were convicted after a long and complex trial involving other Glasgow low-lifers and false testimony, as in the Slater and Meehan cases. Once again Peterhead and the road north beckoned. It took almost twenty years for Campbell and Steele to be freed and cleared. When their conviction was eventually overruled after years of hunger strikes, escapes, publicity stunts and almost countless appeals and appeals on appeals, it emerged that they had been caged, as the tabloids like to say, on concocted police evidence.

Long sentences had been handed down and Campbell, in particular, when in Peterhead embarked on a one-man war against authority. It was always going to end in violence. In June 1986 he was accused of punching a chief officer in the high security prison. The allegation was that he had lashed out with his fist when he heard that a visit from his family had been cancelled because of investigations into a riot the previous night. Such was life in Peterhead at the time. At his trial the judge said he entertained a doubt about the prosecution case and found Campbell not guilty of assault. But at the same time he threw out Campbell's claim that he had been beaten up and kicked by a squad of eight officers in retribution for the riot, resulting in a stomach injury. This was significant as the press at the time was full of stories about so-called "batter squads". In this important case the authorities cleared the prison staff of that particular allegation.

Despite the courts clearing the prison officers in this case it seems undeniable that there were, at the time, what the cons – and their villainous friends outside – called "batter squads" at work in the prison. Many ex-cons have talked to me about this. How much of it was going on will never be fully quantified. Nor will any degree of justification of the behaviour of some prison officers. In a riot there is no referee and no predilection to fight by the Queensberry rules. And back then, inside many parts of prisons, there were no cameras. Conflict is hard on each side and you have to have some sympathy for officers who daily faced the prospect of sudden desperate attacks from men who felt they had nothing to lose, men who were there anyway mostly because of violence when out on the streets.

TC Campbell's health gave concern of a different kind a year or so later. Hunger strikes punctuated his long years behind bars. On this occasion it was a protest against the authorities' plan to move him back to Peterhead after a transfer to Barlinnie. His feuding and fighting up in the North-East fortress had planted a desire in his mind never to see the place again. He had few friends there among prisoners or staff. There was always a lot going on around TC, whatever prison he happened to be in. In this case he went on a "liquids only" diet. He was taken to the prison hospital and given twenty-four-hour care, though the authorities had no plans to force-feed him.

Some will tell you that the pain of Campbell's hunger strikes were on occasion eased with an occasional bar of chocolate or biscuit smuggled to him. You will always find a cynic or two around even in a prison. But if the idea of the hunger strikes were to keep his name in the press then it worked. If lacking in food himself, he provided the newspapers with a rich diet of controversial stories.

As well as turning away any unappetising prison food offered to him, Campbell was busy planning action in the European Court of Human Rights in connection with alleged interference with his mail and other infringements, and won compensation of £250 from the authorities, who were judged to have allowed him to suffer an attack of bed bugs in his cell. Nor was that Peterhead not guilty verdict on the charge of punching an officer the end of that matter. He pursued a claim for damages through the courts and in the autumn of 1989 he was awarded £4,000 against the then Secretary of State for Scotland, Malcolm Rifkind. TC had claimed £40,000 but after three days' evidence a civil jury made the lower award. They said that they were satisfied that Campbell had sustained injuries from the "wrongful action of prison officers." It was admitted on behalf of the Secretary of State that Campbell had suffered a ruptured bowel for which he needed surgery in Aberdeen Royal Infirmary, and that the injury had happened when a number of officers were in his cell.

It was claimed that Campbell had suddenly struck the officer when he told him of the suspended visits. A violent struggle took place in which Campbell and other officers fell together in a heap on the floor. Campbell claimed he was beaten with riot sticks and stamped on. The attacked officer, who was by then retired, said in court that the attack on him was "out of character" and that Campbell had later apologised. He said that Campbell was not involved in the escape bid that had sparked the trouble. A prisoner gave evidence that he had watched through the "Judas hole" in his cell door as warders with sticks beat Campbell.

It is interesting that the officer said that the attack on him was out of character. Way back around the time of his trial for the Bankend Street fire, some of Campbell's associates on the streets had said he was unpredictable – at one moment chatting pleasantly over a pint and then suddenly turning aggressive. A short fuse goes with a life of crime. One day in the company of a celebrated Glasgow hard man I remarked how well we were getting on and he growled, "You have not seen me when the red mist comes down!" The mist that descended on Campbell that day when he heard the bad news of a cancelled family visit was nothing like the grey-white kind that so often flows in from the North Sea to wrap itself round the prison. It was a very bright red.

For Campbell, long years in prisons including the Barlinnie Special Unit lay ahead. There were to be more hunger strikes, more legal battles, more stunts to bring attention to their claims of innocence. Eventually in 2004 the convictions of Campbell and Steele were quashed. So ended the saga of a couple of Peterhead's most recent caged innocents.

6

GENTLE JOHNNY RAMENSKY:
THE GREAT ESCAPER

Few would, or could, disagree with the statement that Peterhead has in its time held the worst of criminals Scotland has produced – murderers, armed robbers, razor slashers, rapists, paedophiles, the irretrievably wicked, and the scum from the slums of the country's great cities. But in an ironic twist of fate it was also for years home to a great patriot and war hero, a man now sadly drifting into forgotten memory, John Ramensky. As "Commando John Ramsay" this boy of Lithuanian descent, who was born in the coalfields of Lanarkshire and grew up in the Gorbals, did his country great and courageous service during the Second World War. But he also wrote himself into criminal history as the most remarkable escaper ever to scale a prison wall in Scotland. Five times he fooled his many Peterhead guards and used his athletic skills to break out of what some would regard as a tartan Alcatraz or Devil's Island. No wall was too high, no lock too secure for this Peterhead legend. The background maketh the man and Gentle Johnny Ramensky was a career criminal who earned his nickname for his acceptance of his fate when his collar was felt by the cops and he normally went gently off to court to take his medicine. He also had the perfect CV for a wartime saboteur and safebreaker.

His early years hardened him for what was to come. His father had come from Lithuania in the late 1890s along with other experienced miners from Eastern Europe. These hard tickets had been hired by Lanarkshire mine owners to help break strikes in the Scottish coal and clay fields. The Scottish mining communities naturally did not take at all well to the newcomers and Johnny grew up in an area where there was bad feeling between Scots and Eastern Europeans. This gave him something of a chip on his shoulder that would last a lifetime.

Johnny's father died when he was eight and he and his mother moved to Glasgow's Gorbals. But there was plenty of time before that at school in Lanarkshire's Glenboig for him to feel prejudice and be at the end of barbs about foreigners and "Poles." Schoolkids and adults used the term as a general derogatory adjective for the incomers, ignoring the fact that many came from other countries like Lithuania and Romania. This was particularly annoying to proud Lithuanians, who reacted as Scots would to being called English!

The feeling of difference from the other kids playing in the muddy fields of Lanarkshire was underlined by the names. Johnny's real name was Yonus Ramanauckus, but a school-teacher arbitrarily changed it to the easier to remember and pronounce Ramensky – though the newspapers often called him Ramenski when his criminal career was at its height. On joining the army in the '40s he changed his name to Ramsay to avoid any further taunting as a foreigner. But to the Glasgow papers and the Glasgow cops he was always Gentle Johnny Ramensky.

Over the years the antagonisms between the two communities in industrial Lanarkshire eased as Scots began to understand that the imported "scabs" had themselves been victims of persecution. Indeed many of them were Jews and Catholics fleeing religious ill-treatment and possible conscription to the Russian army. Others were simply seeking a way out of desperate poverty. When you work shoulder-to-shoulder with a man deep in a dark and dank mine hewing coal or spading clay, there is always a grudging respect that comes from the acceptance of shared danger. But the story of Johnny Ramensky, hero and criminal, also shows that the experience of early days can leave a lifelong mark.

Many a mother has appeared in court to tell judge or sheriff that her boy would have been fine if he had not fallen into bad company. It is unknown if Mrs Ramensky, installed with her family in the infamous Gorbals did that, but it was an excuse that Johnny himself, a man who all his life had a plausible explanation for bad behaviour, used often. He expressed it eloquently in a poignant note, now in the Scottish National Archives, written in Barlinnie in 1951:

Each man has an ambition and I have fulfilled mine long ago. I cherish my career as a safe-blower. In childhood days my feet were planted on the crooked path and took firm root. To each one of us is allotted a niche and I have found mine. Strangely enough, I am happy. For me the die is cast and there is no turning back.

That is as remarkable fifty words or so as you will ever read of a criminal writing about his career. The "crooked path" is real enough, as is his acceptance of a way of life that cost him almost half a century behind bars. His intelligence and sense of reality shine out from his words. It is interesting, too, that he does not mention his heroism as a commando or the undoubted great service he did for his country. The modesty and lack of boastfulness is as striking as it is typical.

A few years ago I went to do some research in and around his childhood home in Glenboig and on a bitter snowy February day I sought the warmth of the fireside in the local pub and the chance to talk to some of the Glenboig natives about the area's most famous son. The young bucks at the bar had barely heard of him, but in the darker corners the older locals talked freely of the man and his reputation. One told me of a return visit Johnny had made to that very bar many years ago to meet up with old friends from school days and when he worked in the local mines. There is still a strong Lithuanian community in the area. Neatly turned out, he looked more like a successful businessman than an infamous criminal. Naturally he was the centre of attention since in these days his name was often splashed across the front pages. On that occasion he drank sparingly, as was his habit, enjoying his fame in a quiet way. But there was no boasting, no playing the big man. No tales of heroism behind the enemy lines fighting with the Italian partisans against the Nazis. He was, as the little note above suggested, a man comfortable with himself. Playing the "wise guy" in a pub was not his style.

Somehow, despite the troubled childhood, he had absorbed a goodish education and was well able to express himself. But that crooked path beckoned and he was barely in long trousers before his collar was first felt by the Glasgow "polis." Minor offences led to more serious burglary and Barlinnie. But even then a certain decency shone through. It was this decency that helped create the nickname Gentle

Johnny. Though part of Glasgow's gangland he was not really a gangster or a violent man. He operated as a sort of freelance specialist opening "sardine cans," as his robber mates called safes, to order for the gangsters themselves. They lacked his skill with explosives and locks, and they were happy enough to pay Johnny well for his services. He did not duff up old ladies to steal their shopping money or pinch their purses. Quite the opposite. It is on record that when after a burglary he examined the spoils and found such as rent books and pension books he popped them in an envelope and went to the post office and returned them to their elderly owners. Jewels and cash, mind you, were a different matter and he had no worries about relieving the wealthy of their worldly goods. But without violence.

His early days in Barlinnie and Saughton were on relatively short sentences before long years in Peterhead came his way as a result of some serious safebreaking in Aberdeen. But one Barlinnie escapade was a dramatic demonstration of the skills that were to stand him in good stead as an escapologist when in the North-East. Bored in jail and resentful about being taunted by his fellow prisoners, mostly from the Glasgow slums, who dismissed him as a wee "Pole," he decided to show them what he could do. Throughout his career he had a true head for heights that could have made him a celebrated Alpinist or circus performer. Outside the jail he was at home on slippery rooftops on dark nights, fearless and, as the cliché has it, cat-like. So one afternoon in the Barlinnie prison exercise yard, on a whim he pulled off his boots, broke away from the escorts and shinned up a rone pipe to emerge high on the roof of the great prison. There he passed an hour or so pleasurably inviting the screws to throw him up a boiled egg or two and walking the roof ridge, high above the yard, like a tightrope walker.

In the 1920s, Barlinnie was overlooked by the tenements of the east end and soon, in the streets with the best views, hundreds gathered to watch the action behind the high walls. Johnny gave them a show to remember. The governor was not happy and prison officers were sent up ladders to coax him down. On their way up they met a fusillade of slates. Next a fire hose was tried in an attempt to dislodge the star of the show. It only added to the sense of farce as, unused for months, it was perished and the officers rather than the prisoner got a soaking. Even one of Johnny's best pals in the prison, a character known as Wee Tommy Clark, was sent up to try to talk sense into him. Johnny told Clark, a lifelong friend, that he was up for a breath of air and might stay a day or two! And the prison chaplain, the Rev. J. McCormack Campbell, was no more successful at persuading him down. Eventually the governor himself took to the ladder and the star climber finally agreed to return to his cell. But it was hunger rather than sweet words that did the trick. A point had been made, even his fellow cons who sneered at him as that "wee Pole" were impressed.

It was all a bit of a laugh. But doing time in Peterhead was less amusing, and here Johnny used his way with words and his compassion to good effect. He had had a narrow scare in the Bar-L in 1930 when he was taken ill with pneumonia and only the prompt action of the prison medic saved him. The doc ruled he was too ill to be treated in prison and he was sent to a nearby hospital, where he recovered. It was a lesson he never forgot and played a part in a long-running battle he had with the Peterhead prison authorities.

In Peterhead his escapes became legendary and are detailed later in this chapter, but in his early years it was prison food and the medical treatment doled out to his fellow inmates that motivated him to go to war with the authorities. Throughout his prison career Johnny was something of a jailhouse lawyer and a friend to cons who did not have his writing skills, skills that were accompanied with a questioning attitude that made him friends as well as enemies in his years inside. Although he had left school at fourteen he was a fluent writer and coherent in argument. He would pick up pencil and paper to plead the case of any con he thought was getting a rough deal and in the Scottish penal system in the 1930s and '40s that meant almost everyone.

He arrived in Peterhead in the early 1930s and it is interesting that the man responsible for his arrest for a safe-blowing in Aberdeen, Superintendent John Westland of the Aberdeen CID, became a lifelong friend. Johnny, like the famous Glasgow Godfather Walter Norval, seemed to regard prison officers and policemen rather like the other side in some sort of criminal game. They did not take it personally. Johnny bore Mr Westland no grudge.

Hardly in the jail, he swiftly started on years of letter-writing. Letters of complaint and special pleading become almost a hobby for many long-term prisoners. They have the time to enter into lengthy correspondence, though many a governor could do without the time-consuming demands of their annoying "pen pals." Johnny's first concern was the treatment of prisoners taken ill in their cells and ending up in the prison hospital. These unfortunates lost their meagre prison wages and with that the chance to buy wee treats like fruit, biscuits or sweets. Johnny wrote forcibly to the governor, pointing out that such "little comforts" were especially important during convalescence.

Whether he won that particular war of words is unclear but he did have some success on other fronts. He was very concerned about the food dished out on special occasions like Christmas. These days in Her Majesty's prisons the important role of a decent healthy diet is acknowledged. What is served up is far from celebrity chef nosh, but it is edible and nutritious, which was not always the case in the '30s. Back then the idea was to sustain life at the minimum of expense and not much else. Locked up when not doing hard labour in the prison quarry there is little else to think about other than the next meal. Johnny was outraged at what was on offer for the Royal Coronation and Jubilee celebrations in the '30s. Although it might puzzle the reader these days why such celebrations were marked in a 1930s nick at all. These days the tabloids like to keep tabs on any special treats and tend to become red-faced with anger, as well as red-topped, at any hint of an extra bar of chocolate or other wee treat for the cons.

In 1937 prisoner 3747 (one Johnny Ramensky) wrote to the governor, Captain J. I. Buchan, as follows:

> *Sir,*
>
> *On Thursday night I was asked which would I like, an apple or an orange, on Coronation Day. I replied neither. Last year on Jubilee Day I was robbed of half my dinner and so were all the other convicts. I was deprived of my beef and I got a half-pound of potatoes instead of a pound. I was given an apple to make it up. The soup that day was rice soup which is horrible and I never eat it. I was starving that day. I wish to protest at the taking away of my food and ask you to consider that if there is any cutting or slicing of diet not to take it away from convicts who are starving enough. I wish to draw to your notice that*

*I lost half my dinner on Jubilee Day and have no desire for a
repitition* [sic] *on Coronation Day.*
   Yours sincerely
   John Ramensky

Johnny was over the years both a persistent headache with
his escapes but also a friend in his later commando days
to Captain Buchan. But his complaint on this occasion was
given short shrift. The prison medical officer wrote in a
report: "The Coronation Day dinner would be 10oz bread,
one pint soup, and 3oz of meat, potatoes and turnip and
an extra 4oz bread and half an ounce of marge. For the
Jubilee dinner there was a deduction of 6oz bread and 8oz
potatoes but an additional 3oz meat and an apple or orange
was given." It was hardly starvation, but as I remarked in
my biography of Johnny (*Gentle Johnny Ramensky*, Black &
White, Edinburgh 2010) it was not quite a celebration dinner
either. And in the climate of prison life in the 1930s it was
perhaps not the cleverest of moves to become known as a
regular complainer even if your letters were more literate
than that of the run-of-the-mill con.

Johnny was in a state of mental turmoil at this time. In
his later years he grew to accept prison life but in this early
long sentence he was prone to depression and that chip on
his shoulder, first placed there in the Glenboig and Gorbals
days, grew heavier by the year. He resented particularly
that the authorities had refused to let him travel to Glasgow
to attend the funeral of his first wife. A letter he wrote in
1937 to the Scottish Home Department is indicative of his
mental state of mind and of conditions in the prison in that
era:

Sir,

I appeal to you for fair play. On 4 Nov 1934 I escaped from Peterhead prison and was caught and thrown into chains. Ever since I have been the victim of petty tyranny and vindictiveness on the part of the governor here. I will relate the latest and you will see for yourself. Bear with me a little and note. On November 1936 the head warder spoke to me in the quarry. He said would you like to be considered for the bathroom job. I replied yes. He said, "Very well, I just thought I would ask you before anyone else asked for the job." He added, of course, you will play the game. The head warder said that's all right then. The bathroom job was not available till Feb 37. In December 36 the head warder again spoke to me in the quarry. He said would I like a job as fireman in the kitchen? I replied no. He said, "You would not like it." He then said all right, of course, and then I have not forgotten the bathroom job. I said that would do me.

On February 10, the day before I was to take over my new job, the head warder told me I was considered an unsuitable person for the job and I could not get it. I saw the governor the next day and stated my case. He admitted the truth of these facts. He told me the reason I did not get the job. He told me that I had written a petition to you [the governor's superiors] *on December last and when I did so a black mark was put against me. I also wish to draw your attention to the fact that in the petition I informed you of the conditions under which a convict by name of Kidd died. By writing to you on that matter I have again angered the governor here. Because he informed me that there was a black mark against me and I was being punished for doing so.*

At the same time yesterday he deprived me of all privileges on a trumped up charge of insolence. A deliberate fake. I have put up with everything these years because I have not proof. I

*have not written to anyone before because things do happen.
But when the governor told me himself I can not do less than
see daylight. I was led on to believe I was getting a change of job.
And in addition I was deprived of privileges. I have been nearly
three years in the quarry. Other men do only a few months or
a year and are then shifted to another job. I do not want a shift.
I only want left alone. Nor do I want to be the victim to the
malice or vindictiveness of the governor here. I trust you will
look into this matter and help the underdog a bit.*

  I am, sir, yours,
  John Ramensky

The reference to work conditions in the quarry is significant.
Speak to any old-timers who worked there and you get a
picture of how grim it was in the '30s. The little train written
about earlier may have looked a tad like *Thomas the Tank
Engine*, so beloved of children's TV, but its passengers were
heading for a hellish day of stone-breaking, hard manual
labour of the sort that most folk of the time fiercely believed
was due punishment, however severe, for lawbreakers.
The convicts slaved in all weathers, under the vigilant eyes
of guards armed with rifles and cutlasses, to cut the stone
to make those massive blocks for the harbour breakwater.
When you visualise the conditions and what it must have
been like, you understand the desire of the prisoners to get
out of the quarry and into a relatively cushy job in the prison
hospital or the tailors' shops. Or maybe even an attendant in
the bathroom.

This was not the first time Johnny had taken up his pen
in the interests of Prisoner Kidd. In December 1934 he had
written to the governor in the following terms:

Sir,

I wish to draw to your attention to the conditions under which a convict has to fight for his life when attacked with pneumonia. Yesterday, Friday, December 4, convict Kidd died of pneumonia. I do not say he died for want of attention, but I do think he died for the lack of proper treatment and the care of those most competent to look after him. When he died, convict Kidd was in the care of a prison warder. The warder does his best. At least I hope so. But even his best, after all, does not mean very much. I bring this to your notice hoping you can do something to give a convict a chance. The same chance as every other prisoner receives in other prisons. Speaking personally, from experience, when I was unlucky enough to contract pneumonia in Barlinnie in 1931, I was immediately rushed to Lightburn Hospital, Shettleston. If I had been kept in Barlinnie I would never have pulled through. So I also believe Kidd would have pulled through. The brightness and hope one meets in hospital helps wonderfully. The drabness of the surroundings in prison does not help a convict in his fight for life. I therefore ask you to advocate that when a convict is seriously ill to send him outside to the care of those who are highly proficient in this matter. I lay this subject before you and trust that you will give it your earnest consideration.

I am sir, etc.

This is an intelligent, compassionate letter and its main point – that seriously ill prisoners should be given prompt and expert medical attention – cannot be contested. But the "earnest consideration" given to it was not what Johnny expected. The governor and the medical officer were more concerned with what they thought was a slur on them rather than the circumstances of poor Kidd's death. They considered legal action. You can't help but think that in similar circumstance these days it would be the other way around and m'learned friends would have to be consulted forthwith by the relatives of the deceased and compensation sought through the courts. And probably awarded.

However, Johnny Ramensky all these years ago was not going to be scared off or pushed aside. The deaths of prisoners in custody became something of an obsession with him and he regularly used his skill as a "jailhouse lawyer" in letters to the authorities on the subject. Far from being cowed at the threat of legal action against him he got bolder as he went along. The original Kidd letter was followed by this one:

Sir,

Last December I wrote to you a petition concerning the death of a convict name Kidd. I received your answer "no reason for taking action". Since then another convict named Gray died. I wish to draw your attention to the fact that his death was caused through neglect. Frank Gray reported sick on Sunday 21st but received no treatment. On Monday 22nd he again complained of not feeling well. The doctor told him there was nothing wrong with him and gave him two aspirins. On Tuesday 23rd Gray had to be admitted to hospital. He was kept there some time and finally sent outside to some infirmary. He died there. If ordinary precautions had been taken by the authorities here, that man's life could have been saved.

He was kept waiting so long in hope of treatment and then too long in the prison hospital that the man had no chance. The only good thing I can see is that he was allowed to die outside of prison. The food here is very bad and a convict has no stamina to fight an illness.

Ramensky went on to point out that Gray had been serving five years and added that the longer a person was held in Peterhead the greater the effect on his general health. Again he asked "for steps to be taken." His prison correspondence, held in the National Archives, shows a penchant for ending letters with various versions of "I trust you will act." No doubt composing these wordy epistles kept his mind active, but there is little evidence that they did much to change conditions in any of the many hard places in which he was held.

The one notable exception is that Ramensky was largely responsible for ending the barbaric practice of shackling prisoners in iron restraints. He was, in this era of the '30s, big news in the papers, and when he was shackled after being caught following one of his escapes it made headlines. The thought of "Gentle Johnny" in chains upset the readers and, more importantly, angered MPs and do-gooders of all stripes. The fuss was such that the authorities had a black-smith go to his Peterhead cell and cut him free and from that day on no shackles were used in Scottish prisons. It was a major victory in the battle for humane treatment of offenders. Without the Ramensky effect, shackling people in irons might have continued on for years. His celebrity was the key to the end of this horrible, almost medieval, practice.

Johnny's prolific letter-writing on behalf of those taking ill in prison is particularly ironic in that his own life ended in a similar incident, though on this occasion, despite a certain amount of controversy, there can be no serious criticism of his jailers. In November 1972 he was serving his final sentence in Perth Prison, a broken man, a shadow of the figure who had left Peterhead in the 1940s to train as a commando in the Lochaber hills, fight alongside partisans in Italy and after the war spend years running darkened rooftops en route to blowing yet another safe. He had been arrested earlier in the year in Ayr hiding behind a chimney, and not long before he had fallen from a building in Stirling in the act of avoiding the cops. He sustained serious injuries in this fall, was hospitalised and appeared in court as a tragic figure in a wheelchair. His friends felt that he never fully recovered.

On the weekend of his death he was, on the Friday afternoon, doing some "light work," as the Perth Prison official report described it (sorting mail bags for the Post Office), with a party of fellow prisoners and to help pass the time the cons were playing a friendly game of "Wordie," a sort of Scrabble in which little slips of paper were passed round and the players added letters and tried to create words. It was a game popular in prisons in the days before electronic entertainment. The tragedy of his final hours was told to me in detail by Willie Leitch, a famous ex-con who had become over the years a close friend of Johnny. Willie himself had been a jailbreaker and like Johnny he had a service background, though Willie was a Navy man rather than a commando.

When Willie told me about the game of Wordie I remarked that Johnny, with his passion for letter-writing and words, would run out an easy winner. With a twinkle in his eye Willie told me, "Not necessarily – there were a lot of clever folk in Perth prison that day!" But although most of the players were in good humour looking forward to the break in routine that the weekend brought, Johnny was low, complaining of a headache. He put down the increasing frequency of his headaches to the odd whack with a police baton down the years or the after effect of his Stirling fall. He was rubbing his head and, according to Willie, there was a red patch moving across the side of his face. His fellow Wordie players became so worried, although he insisted he was all right, they thought that he needed looked at and they summoned Sandy Bain, a popular warder who before joining the prison service was in the RAF. Sandy decided that Johnny should be taken back to his cell for a lie down and the cell was kept unlocked so that the warders could keep an eye on him. The prison surgery was involved and it soon became clear that something serious was wrong. Johnny was bleeding from the mouth and confused, talking to himself. In contrast to the Peterhead situation with convicts Kidd and Gray back in the '30s, prompt action was taken to send Johnny to Perth Royal infirmary.

He died there less than twenty-four hours later. Somehow or other in every prison the inmates quickly learn what is going on. No newsletters are handed out but any event of significance soon spreads throughout the jail. Willie Leitch remembers that the whole place fell silent when news of Johnny's death got around. "Even the mice must have known something was wrong," he told me.

Gentle Johnny's final resting place is Lambhill Cemetery in Glasgow. I visited it with his great-grandson, Haig Ferguson, and his great-granddaughter, Kendal, two youngsters Johnny would have been immensely proud of, and we felt sadness that there was nothing in this almost derelict, vandalised and melancholy place to pay tribute to one of the most remarkable Scots of the twentieth century. His headstone, like hundreds of others around it, lay toppled over in lank grass, the green dulled by polluted city air. Johnny

Ramensky was called by some a common criminal yet he was a man who, before he died, had managed to capture the public's imagination and affection. And a man who played an extraordinary role in the fight against the Nazis.

Johnny's life change came about when he served in Italy with General Lucky Laycock's commandos after volunteering to join the army. No doubt his ability as an escaper played a role in attracting the attention of the Secret Services and eased his way into the commandos, turning him temporarily from criminal safebreaker to war hero.

As earlier recounted, when in Barlinnie he showed his climbing skills, his head for heights and the agility to scale prison walls. But he did not break out from the Glasgow prison and when in Lightburn Hospital he did not take advantage of his surroundings to do a runner and avoid a return to his cell. In Peterhead he was unsettled, bored and felt he was victimised. So he thumbed his nose at the authorities with frequent escapes and became a nightmare for his captors. At one stage it was joked that visitors should first check whether he was inside or outside before they called on the prison.

In his five escapes he never managed to travel more than a few dozen miles from the prison before recapture. This I suspect was largely because the escapes were symbolic, a way of making a protest that generated headlines rather than a desire to head away from the prison to a life on the run. Each escape was its own reward. If ever a man was in the category of what the prison authorities describe as high escape risk it was John Ramsay – aka John Ramenski, aka Johnny Ramensky, aka Yonus Ramanauckas.

The record book says it all:

November 1934 – Twenty-nine hours at large
August 1952 – Recaptured the following day
February 1958 – Recaptured the following day
October 1958 – Recaptured the following day
December 1958 – Around nine days at large

The only other prisoner to come near his record is a John Burnside, who managed to get over the wall five times from different Scottish jails – but "only" three times from Peterhead. So Johnny can, most would agree, claim to be the Great Escaper.

The details of his various escapes give an intriguing insight to life in the prison before and after the Second World War. It took more than gymnastic skill to get out of Peterhead. In the early '30s one prisoner had, as recounted earlier, made an escape from a quarry work party and was shot by a guard as he tried to run for freedom, but Johnny managed to get out from inside as it were. It was a remarkable feat. To make it at all possible you have to consider the construction of the prison. The walls were made from thick stone blocks that inevitably had little ledges, handholds and footholds that could assist a climber. You only have to look at the many mountaineering books with photographs of sheer rock faces worldwide that have been conquered by climbers to see that some of them look impossible to scale, but it can be done. These days most prison walls are smooth, any possible holds cemented over and the wall topped with barbed wire. And nowadays the weak point in holding prisoners is the travelling to and from courts and jails by car and van, but the old walls of Peterhead, first erected in the 1880s, could be climbed by a brave expert – and in Johnny's first escape that is what many think happened.

The newspaper reports of the time are short on detail but they do point out that Ramensky was a man of great physical strength and cunning. The anger generated by the refusal of the authorities to allow him to attend the funeral of his wife back in Glasgow had also given him a steely determination. The timing of the escape was not wisely chosen, however, as November in North-East Scotland is a time of bitter cold, strong winds off the North Sea and long periods of rain, sleet and snow. But to Ramensky the weather was not a factor – he simply wanted to get out at any time in any conditions. He would show the authorities what he was like. He was dressed in a prison suit of brown moleskin with long trousers and a battledress-style jacket. Instead of the good pair of boots he would have needed outside in the frequent snowstorms, he wore light black shoes. The escape was made between six and seven in the morning when the place was busy with the hustle of serving breakfast to hundreds of cons. A fellow prisoner told me that in the enquiry into how he had got out it was postulated that he had simply hurled himself up the outside prison wall as far as he could go and hung silently there by his hands for a half hour or so, unseen by any passing warders, before finally clambering further up the rough wall and over the top. No ladders or grappling ropes were found anywhere near the scene. It was an astonishing demonstration of raw climbing skill and determination – though it should be pointed out that some of the warders were incredulous that he could have escaped that way, and you will still get some who tell you that in his escapes he hid in the empty sacks of a coal lorry rather than climb the walls in what was to become a legendary way.

However, what happened next was an early example of what was to happen during later escapes. Johnny may have put a great deal of planning into his actual breakouts but little on what to do once he was on the outside. This first escape sparked a massive manhunt. Farms were searched by the cops who were out in force, road junctions watched and hundreds of folk going about their business were quizzed. He managed to reach Ellon, where he encountered a problem. The bridge there, over the river Ythan, was blocked at both ends and was under scrutiny by a posse of lawmen. There seemed no way to get to the other side unseen, but the determined Ramensky made it! He crawled under the bridge and swung his way, undetected and Tarzan-like, on the metal and stone framework to the other side. Once over the river he found a hiding place in a garage loft to wait for the cold darkness to descend. After a few hours he was on the move and he swam and stumbled across the near-frozen waters of a tributary of the Ythan, heading for another village, but he was finally spotted in a field near Foveran.

The police gave chase across open ground. There was only one ending to this and after almost two days without food the quarry was weakened and stricken. He had an iron bar in his hand but surrendered without violence, and it was said that he even joked with his pursuers. It all added to the legend of Gentle Johnny. By now you suspect that a prison meal, however basic, and a cell with a blanket looked more attractive than another night in the dark and cold.

The determination behind his next escape was likewise fuelled by a feeling that he was hard done to by society in general. It came in 1952 when he was back in Peterhead. He had on ending his previous Peterhead sentence in 1943 volunteered to join the army and play a role in the defeat of fascism. There is a myth that he was freed from prison early on condition that he helped the war effort with his safe-blowing expertise. Not so. Documents held in the National Archives show clearly that he served his sentence and then joined up. Aware of his skills, the authorities were quick to recognise his use to the commandos as a saboteur as well as a safecracker. So he joined up and did training in the hills of Lochaber and won himself the right to wear the famed Green Beret.

His ability to be of help to the war effort should not be underestimated. For a period after training he toured army establishments, lecturing on how to break into highly-guarded establishments and how to open safes that contained secret plans and other useful information. It is somewhat ironic that a man who forswore violence, despite a lifetime of crime, was trained by the army in the black arts of combat, armed and unarmed. How to kill silently was a vital part of the good commando's armoury.

The great commander Lucky Laycock – tasked by Churchill to create the commandos – admired his skills and bravery and was responsible for recruiting him. After training Ramensky was parachuted behind enemy lines to fight with Italian partisans and to break into safes belonging to Rommel and Goering. On demob he got a warm letter from Laycock thanking him for his war efforts. These two were, as they say, unlikely bedfellows but there seems to have been a real sense of friendship between them. This friendship was typical Ramensky, for he also became close to the Peterhead governor J. I. Buchan despite being a total "pest" to the prison service with his constant letters of complaints and his penchant for going over the heads of his Peterhead jailors to politicians and to those at the top of the prison service in Edinburgh. Another friend who got postcards from him during the war was the aforementioned top Aberdeen cop John Westland, who had, as we saw, on occasion helped put him behind bars!

A former Aberdeen journalist, Harvey Grainger, remembers his father, who also worked for the *Press and Journal* in the 1930s, telling him how Ramensky used to return from an escape or one of his adventures in the commandos with a wee present or two for friends in the police. There was some sort of psychological bonding going on. Jim Ironside, a former officer in Peterhead, told me that Ramensky even on occasion sent a Christmas card to "The staff, HP Prison Peterhead." Maybe that is not so surprising, as Johnny often referred to various prisons as "my second home." But it was pretty surprising – not many old lags keep their jailors on their Christmas card list!

But the real tragedy of Ramensky is that with the war over he could not settle down on the right side of the law despite offers of help from prison governors, local businessmen and even some top cops who had felt his collar in the years leading up to the war. He needed the excitement of running darkened rooftops seeking ready cash. But it was that thrill that he seemed to need most. His ill-gotten gains usually went quickly on gambling. But there was always another safe to open in search of more readies to blow at the bookies or the dog tracks of Glasgow. So here he was again back in Peterhead after being nabbed blowing a safe in Cardonald, Glasgow.

His second escape, in August 1952, was not quite the mystery of the first back in the '30s. This time he had a semi-trusted job in the prison hospital and somehow or other got out of his cell on to the roof of the prison (roofs seemed to have had an attraction for him, inside or out of jail) and then to the yard below before using his climbing skills to get outside undetected. It was thought that his skill with locks had allowed him to open his cell door. He had also cunningly laid a dummy in his bed and that fooled the staff long enough to delay the alarm being called. The hunt for him was led by Fred Shepard of the North-East counties force but the fame of the fugitive, by now burnished by the extensive newspaper stories of his war service, was such that all police forces in Scotland were alerted to the fact that he was on the run. The cops knew a man of his initiative was as likely to turn up in Orkney or Dumfries as Aberdeen. But there was no need for a countrywide manhunt – he was picked up not all that far from the prison at Balmedie after forty-seven hours of freedom.

In January 1958 he wrote himself into the record books with a third escape. But this time he took the easy way in that he had the help of a ladder to scale the walls. He was well used by now to being a sort of human fox in a chase, but this time it was a bit different – dogs as well as men were after him. A local couple had an interest in bloodhounds and a few good specimens at the ready. They offered their animals to help find Johnny, the first time Scottish police had used such dogs, which are normally associated with sniffing out escapers from jails in the American Deep South. For the police and prison authorities to use such methods in the hunt for an escaper was certainly unusual. Ramensky was making police and prison authorities look foolish, if not incompetent, with the regularity of his escapes, and so anything was worth a try.

It has to be said a charge of incompetence against the authorities may well stand up in this case. It is not a good idea to leave ladders around a prison. Again it was early morning with the staff and prisoners preoccupied with breakfast when he spotted a chance. With no one around he managed to climb a thin gas pipe he had noticed that disappeared upwards near a skylight. He was now three storeys up in a bitter cold dawn but getting to ground level outside the walls of the building was not the same challenge as getting into the loft in the first place. Dropping down a rone pipe was easier than climbing the gas pipe.

On the ground a certain lack of security was demonstrated by the fact that he could, undetected, pick the lock of a shed which contained a ladder. It was not a long one but tall enough to get him within grasping distance of the top of the eighteen-feet high wall. It was a classic spur-of-the-moment escape, not something that had been planned for weeks or months. Over the wall Johnny's only thought was to put distance between himself and the prison, and again there was no master plan, no getaway car with a bunch of pals waiting for him.

But as he made his careful way from the vicinity of the prison searching for every spot of cover he could find, the northern morning was lightening and four maltmen from a nearby distillery saw him fleeing and raised the alarm. But to use the patois of the North-East, the distillery men told the cops that the prisoner had "jouket" them and disappeared over a dry stone wall. However, the area where he had been spotted was ideal for the bloodhounds to pick up his scent and they duly did so. But Johnny had headed off to cross the main road and when the dogs got there they became confused by all the other smells around – petrol from cars, pedestrian scents and the messy evidence of farm animals who had passed this way. The dogs lost the trail. What had seemed a good idea at the time was not, in practice, working.

However, the daughter of the grieve at Dales Home Farm, less than a mile from the jail, had noticed a man she did not know in the area, though she did not mention it to her mother till some time later. Little Gladys Krowcyk, only eight, was unaware of the manhunt. The usual massive search of barns and sheds, any possible hiding place, went on – it was becoming something of a routine!

The day of this escape was market day in Aberdeen and many a farmer heading for a profitable visit to the auction ring, and later the pub, had his drouthy plans delayed by roadblocks. But the man on the run had no chance with no money, nowhere to stay and no plan. He was picked up in Peterhead after twenty-eight hours, despite an attempt at disguise wearing prison warder's clothes he had stolen from the shed where he had found the ladder.

Escape number four followed the routine: break out followed by manhunt, particularly in farms. In some of his previous escapes Johnny had shown a penchant for taking the odd nap in straw bales, undeterred by farmyard smells, mice or rats. In the inclement weather of these parts the straw at least provided some welcome warmth and a place to rest. His pursuers spent hours energetically stabbing hayforks into straw bales. This time he was out from a Friday to a Sunday before being spotted in a nearby farm. Again a youngster was involved. This time it was a seven-year-old, wee David Smith, who played a role in his recapture.

The lad had gone into one of the barns on the family farm with one of the farm workers and being a bright spark, he noticed the bales had been disturbed. He climbed on to them and turned to his companion with a shout: "Ramensky is here!" It is a dramatic illustration of Ramensky's fame that even a seven-year-old recognised him immediately.

Interestingly, wee Davie's companion was one George Henderson who, when a distillery worker, had been involved in the recapture of the Great Escaper in one of his earlier adventures. Ramensky would have done well to find out the whereabouts of Mr Henderson so that he could avoid him before he made yet another escape! Wee David later told a bevy of reporters, many of whom had covered other Ramensky escapes, that, "I saw Ramensky lying among the bales and he said, 'You should not have come in here, sonny,' and I shouted to Mr Henderson that I was frightened but that Ramensky has said, 'Don't be scared, sonny, I won't hurt you.'" Gentle Johnny once again.

George Henderson tried to get the fugitive to give up there and then but he refused and in a pathetic scene watched by the boy, he pleaded for "just a five-minute start." David's father later told reporters that Johnny looked old and decrepit and they could not bring themselves to use force against him. One foot was bruised and bleeding, with a dirty bandage roughly tied round it. George Henderson stayed with the Great Escaper while the farmer went to the prison to inform the authorities. As they walked together Johnny pathetically pleaded just to be left alone but they soon came to a spot where the cops were watching out for him. He made one last attempt to hide behind a wall but when he saw Inspector John Campbell and a constable named Hendry he surrendered, the game was up.

The next escape, his fifth, was more interesting and mysterious than the rather sad antics at the Smith farm. This time he was out for almost nine days. And the mystery is that when captured he was clean-shaven, looking well fed and chipper. Not at all like the exhausted, shambolic and beaten man who surrendered at the conclusion of his fourth escape. Was he given shelter and food by, as a local newspaper speculated, "a kind-hearted but misguided local"? His commando training would have helped him live off the land and in particular he was said to be an expert in guddling trout. But clean-shaven? Neatly dressed? It is hardly likely that a razor and soap was part of his kit when he escaped.

There are those who think his good looks and charm enabled him to get help from a local woman who knew his fame and took a fancy to him. Not unlikely, as he was almost a legend in the area, but the man himself was giving nothing away and smilingly remarked he was keeping the real story for his autobiography! But he never got to write it and the mystery of where he was and who, if anyone, helped him remains.

But his fame and recognisability could work against him as well as in his favour. This time a lorry driver had recognised him at a roadside and called the cops and yet another manhunt was to end with the Great Escaper huckled head down in the back of a police car heading for Peterhead Prison. Back in the jail Johnny would face court action after his escapes, but he was not the only man in trouble. One of the legendary governors of the great prison was Duncan Mackenzie, who ruled the jail from 1958 to 1961. Johnny was so popular in the area that at court appearances crowds would watch him arrive and depart and cheer him with shouts of "Good old Johnny."

Mr Mackenzie was not such a fan. Ramensky was a permanent headache to him and his bosses in Edinburgh took a dim view of the escapes. The governor even told him to present himself down in the capital to be given a severe wigging about security. Johnny and his highly-publicised escapades were making the prison something of a national laughing stock. He was not to be allowed to escape again. Full stop. No more lurid newspaper headlines about jail-breaks and reports in the papers about lax security were to be allowed. The solution was to have him watched twenty-four/seven. Six officers were specially selected to keep an eye on him at all times. That is heavy-duty security. Even Johnny came to accept that under such conditions he had to become the Great Escaper (Retired).

It is interesting that Mr Mackenzie, the soft-spoken son of a Highland crofter, was wise in the ways of the prison service and despite the trouble Ramensky had caused him down the years he developed a friendship with him and tried hard to get him to change his ways, a hopeless task.

Johnny also had a mixed relationship with two other governors – Major D.C. Heron-Watson and, of course, Captain J. I. Buchan. Both found him at times a nightmare prisoner, a constant headache, a world-class all-round pest. But both also had a sneaking admiration for him. Heron-Watson showed kindness in allowing him to keep a diary and was rewarded with another rap over the knuckles from his superiors in Edinburgh and, of course, Buchan played a major role in getting him into the army and he got his reward in postcards from the front from the commando, and on occasion even a wee present sent from abroad.

All governors, men of ability, recognised that Johnny was something special. A captive like no other they would meet in a career in the prison service. Indeed, in his final years in Perth prison documents show that he was still on the records as a potential escaper, though in reality his days of spectacular and unauthorised departures from prison premises were long over. But the thought remains that for any governor, their own Great Escape would have been to be given control of a prison that did not contain Commando Johnny Ramensky. That would be a posting that at least would guarantee the governor would get a good night's sleep, unworried about whether or not Gentle Johnny Ramensky was still in his cell.

7

BLEAK TALES FROM A BANK ROBBER
AND GODFATHER

The Peterhead experience, as endured from behind cold iron bars, has never been a remotely pleasant one. Mental misery and despair and physical deprivation goes with the territory. From day one those incarcerated paid a high price for their crimes, separated from family and denied the comfort of the company of their like-minded villains and cohorts on the outside. Society was making them pay for their evil deeds with a regime that meant punishment was just that – day after grinding day. For the majority of its existence Peterhead punishment could be broken down to, obviously, loss of freedom, poor food, inadequate medical care and warders who on occasion could be as violent as their charges. Home comforts there were none. The outcasts who toiled in the quarries in the early days, under the barrels of rifles wielded by potentially trigger-happy warders and civilian guards, suffered back-breaking work in a hostile climate during the day and returned to cold fare, hopelessness, darkness, rough blankets and hard mattresses at night.

The soundtrack to such a miserable life was not the latest hits from an MP3 player or a TV in your cell. In the frequent foggy weather it was the mournful howling of what the prisoners called the Boddam Coo. This was no smelly four-legged grass muncher, but one of Scotland's most iconic lighthouses, built in 1827 by Robert Stevenson on the wind-swept and bleak Buchan Ness. Its red and white stripes could be seen for miles around and its well-used foghorn could be heard from the prison and for miles out to sea and inland too to the rich farmlands of Aberdeenshire. For cons up from the industrial Central Belt it was a memory of another way of life in an area far removed from the polluted air and dark tenements of Glasgow, a memory that the hard men took home when the prison doors finally opened for them. It was rather different from the other persistent aural memory of the cons – the constant dispiriting clang of cell doors and the scratch of keys in locks.

It was only towards the end of the long life of the institution that such things as training in a trade, some degree of compassion, and attempts to combine retribution and redemption were given more than a passing thought. It was yet another reminder of the irony that the high-minded intention of building a lifesaving harbour also led to hell on earth for thousands of Scots convicts. No music and concerts from local musicians in these days. But Johnny Cash's anthem to San Quentin, another infamous prison thousands of miles away across the world, would have been recognised by any inmate:

> *San Quentin, I hate every inch of you*
> *You've cut me and scarred me thru' and thru'*

First-hand accounts of the life of early prisoners are scarce, but in the later years, the 1940s onwards, criminals of a literary bent – not as rare as you might imagine – put pencil to scrap paper to record what it was really like. And I had the good fortune to get the chance to write biographies of two of Scotland's most remarkable criminals – Johnny Ramensky, of course, and Glasgow's first Godfather, Walter Norval. Their insight into day-to-day life in Peterhead was intriguing. Both had wide experience of many of Scotland's jails, but Peterhead was like no other.

Walter Norval spent almost a decade inside "PHead," as he often called it, serving terms for different serious crimes. The use of the name "PHead" was fairly common with Glasgow cons, though some would refer to it as "PHeid." The old jail, as we have seen, attracted many nicknames in its time: The Hate Factory, Scotland's Gulag, COLDitz, etc. But the fact that many of the staff were "loons frae Aberdeenshire" – though their guests mostly came from outside the area – gave rise to another local nickname: "the napper." This came from the Doric name for a person's head – his napper. It was an easy linguistic jump from Peterhead to "the napper."

There must have been some fun conversations between cons and warders at times, as the local North-East dialect is alien to those who reside in the Lowlands. Though to be fair there are plenty around who also find a Glesca dialect a tad difficult to understand. The Doric is on the verge of being a separate language. The scope for misunderstanding is enormous. I remember being on a long overseas trip to Canada as a young journalist with a group of hacks which included a worthy from the *Press and Journal* newsroom. Late at night after a few drams had been taken to ease the tension of the day – at least that was our excuse – a favourite entertainment was for us to ask Jim to "talk Aberdonian" and we would try to guess what he was saying. Notwithstanding the effect of the grog, sometimes we got it very wrong.

In his later years back in Glasgow, Norval retained an appetite for porridge as served in places well kent to him like Barlinnie and Polmont Borstal, as well as Peterhead. Writing his life story with me he used to share a plate of porridge as he reminisced on his time up north. (I enjoyed that spoonful or two cooked up by himself, a wee treat that enabled me to joke that I had done "porridge" with the infamous Glasgow Godfather!)

His tales were mostly bleak. But he could recount a few moments of kindness, an occasional gentle side, shown by those who kept him incarcerated. One such story was of arriving back in the jail in Aberdeenshire after a period of freedom on the streets of his native city. On his arrival one veteran officer, recognising him from the '60s, greeted him with the friendly remark: "Come on, Wattie, you're home again." The kindly officer took this feared denizen of Glasgow's post-war gangland to the laundry, where almost immediately among the workers there he met another familiar face. This was a con called Willie Bennett aka "the Wee Red Devil." This was the lawbreakers' humour at is best – the moniker did not refer to Manchester United or Third Lanark or indeed any red-shirted football team. It was a tag with a more sinister side. The red referred to was blood and was a wry acknowledgement of the amount Willie had spilled on the streets of Govan on the banks of the Clyde. This meeting with Bennett was a bonus for Walter, who was given that permanent goal of the gangster – respect – by Willie. Handshakes and small talk over, Norval collected clean sheets and a pillow and was given an assurance that his laundry would get first-class attention and his prison uniform, his towels and his bed linen would be looked after in a fitting style for gangland royalty.

No one in any nick lives quite the life of a captured gangster as shown in that enjoyable movie *The Italian Job* (the 1969 version, not the remake), where Noel Coward memorably lounged around in a velvet dressing gown and comfy slippers as fellow cons jumped to his command and made sure any little luxuries went his way. Mind you, Norval came as close to it as anyone in Peterhead and fellow jailbirds would make his sandwiches and boil the water for his tea, maybe even add the sugar and stir it for him, and run little errands round the jail at his behest. Inside he was a man sometimes to be feared and always to be given a full measure of that so desired "respect."

The extent of this was demonstrated to me in his later years as he sat in a comfy armchair in his Possilpark flat, surrounded by memorabilia of his beloved Celtic Football Club, and told me in detail about the early hours of this second stay in Peterhead. From the laundry he was escorted to his cell on the third landing of "A" hall. Around him the cells were filled with old mates from the Polmont Borstal days (another reminder that that hard place where teenagers were held in punishing circumstances was mostly a failure in its task of setting these tenement tearaways on to a life led within the law). These by now veteran criminals held "up north" greeted his return to their fold with gifts. The presents he was handed were a selection of the little everyday items that smoothed out the long days and nights in jail. No Christmas Day-style leather gloves, aftershave, silk shirts in these tributes, but tea bags, sugar, sweets, biscuits, books and the like were very much welcomed.

In telling me of his welcome Walter reminisced and painted an intriguing picture of life in Peterhead around half a century ago. He was still able to be a manipulative figure in the prison society, helping to organise football leagues and other sports. This, and long sweaty hours in the gym or on the football field, was his way of easing the pain of confinement. Others in his prison circle indulged themselves in a hobby, painting or writing. He remembered a night when the infamous Walter Scott Ellis sent a message for Norval to call in to his cell when allowed by what the cons called the "screws." Scott Ellis, a Glasgow criminal legend, had a particular hatred for the police, not feelings Norval completely shared. Indeed in his early days as a criminal he had some sort of friendship with the cops who were always on his tail. This was a different attitude to that of Scott Ellis and his cohorts such as John "Bat" Neeson and John McIntyre (aka Mac the Knife) who had all been caged, as the Glasgow tabloids like to say, for bank robbery. They HATED the "bluebottles," as Walter called the cops. Incidentally Neeson's nickname had nothing to do with skills with a baseball bat, as you might expect from his background, but was a comment on his eyesight.

The one commodity the prisoner has in spades is time. We all remember visits to dusty museums in our youth to look in wonder at ships in bottles and examine walrus tusks engraved with full-rigged ships and the like. Prisons show that true art can emerge when raw talent and endless time are given full reign. The therapeutic effects of painting, sculpture and poetry and short story writing came to full fruition in Scotland in that famous penal experiment that briefly and brightly flourished in Barlinnie and was known worldwide as the Special Unit. There, inmates like Jimmy

Boyle and Hugh Collins made names for themselves in the art world. The art discussed by Scott Ellis and Walter that night in Peterhead over a cup of tea was not the grand stuff of such as Boyle with his Edinburgh Festival exhibitions. It was much less fashionable.

Scott Ellis had a hobby once immensely popular but now largely forgotten, marquetry, where inlayed and carefully cut and shaped pieces of wood varnished in various colours produced an image – a sort of painting in wood. Ellis enjoyed it and over the years had become highly skilled. The reason for this particular visit to Norval's cell was because he was intent on making a piece of marquetry work for his friend "Wattie." Walter was given the honour of choosing the subject and he requested a scene from Dickens, the Old Curiosity Shop. Ellis, time no object, toiled for months to produce two versions. Walter sent one to someone on the outside as a gift, the other he kept. That was back in 1977 and Walter Norval proudly shows it to anyone interested who drops by to this day. The complexity of the piece is remarkable. A shop window is filled with pottery and gifts and an old man, dressed in top hat and Victorian clothes, stands outside gazing in. It is not an easy subject but it is beautifully executed.

Scott Ellis was infamous in the Glasgow crime scene but he was far from the only hard man with an interest in art who found himself caged. As mentioned, Jimmy Boyle's talent for sculpture is legendary, as was the ability of Hugh Collins to translate his gangland experiences into book form. But these two were exceptional – fawned on by some in the art world who revelled in a connection with men who had swum in dirty violent waters far removed from the warm white wine and canapés of the normal art gallery. Other prisoners unknown to the general public scribbled poetry or made sketches of their surroundings often in stark black and white.

Norval made me a present of an interesting piece of work as a souvenir of our time writing his life story – a splendid model of a full-rigged galleon made by Billy Manson, a jailbird friend. This product of many hours' work carries its name proudly on its wooden stand and, in a classic example of prison humour, the legend reads . . . *HMS Injustice*. Aye, that'll be right, as they say in Glasgow.

The Barlinnie Special Unit was of course the most significant of what some think of as the "reform through art movement." In time the authorities turned against it as just too much of a soft touch for violent criminals and closed the unit down, though some of its pioneering ideas continued in a diluted form in other prisons. And in 2013 an organisation called Theatre Nemo, founded by a remarkable woman called Isobel McCue, is doing sterling work in Scottish prisons using music, dance, drumming and drawing to encourage prisoners who have never been exposed to such matters to engage with the arts while inside and follow up that interest when released. In particular the organisation tries to help those with mental problems while behind bars. The pioneers of the Special Unit would have greatly approved of Isobel and her friends and co-workers. Some of the best stuff Theatre Nemo students have produced is in the form of visual novels and "comic book" magazines. The stark images – and the humour – of prison life is brilliantly demonstrated in their occasional exhibitions held in places such as Barlinnie.

But Norval's chats in PHead with other cons were not always on matters artistic. Old memories of criminal ploys were recalled time after time. Walter Norval and Scott Ellis had much experience of criminal life in Glasgow. One cop they shared some antagonism over was a Glasgow detective called Norman Walker, who was said to have told some dubious tales about Scott Ellis that had resulted in a conviction and a long sentence. Walker said he was on a day off in a district where a bank robbery had just happened and he chanced into the vicinity to see three men leaving a car and taking off. The men he said he saw were Scott Ellis, Bat Neeson and Mac the Knife. Walker said he was in the area to buy a sheet of glass to repair a window at his house. It might have seemed dodgy and too much of a coincidence but the jury swallowed it.

The long nights as the cold North-East winds swirled round the prison walls, and often the Boddam Coo growled mournfully in the background, were ideal for sharing old memories. Norval remembers one night in the jail and a tale of guns – an area where he had interest and expertise as an armed robber – that made him laugh. The story was of a Glasgow gangster, "tooled up," as they say, being pursued through one of the city's many fine parks by a couple of determined young cops. The cops were faster over the ground than the bad guy and he realised he had to get rid of his gun before they nabbed him. He figured out it was no use just tossing it into the bushes or a nearby stream – metal detectors would soon find it. Instead he climbed to the top of the tallest tree he could see and taped the weapon to the uppermost branch. When the area of the chase was later swept by the cops using the detectors, they strolled past the tree without a clue of what its branches, high above them, hid!

Back in the North-East, facing around a decade behind

bars for attempted murder, Walter Norval met up with old acquaintances from the other side of prison life – the warders. Norval's transfer to Peterhead this time after an initial spell in Barlinnie gives a flavour of prison life in that era. The van transferring him from Barlinnie halted at Craiginches in Aberdeen, where he was held in one of the "dog boxes" – cells not much bigger than a broom cupboard. He had hoped that Craiginches would be his final destination since the regime there was considered less arduous than in Peterhead. He sat in the darkness and eventually he heard the bolt drawn. At the other side of the door was a well-kent face, Mr James Frazer. Known as "Jim'll Fix It," Mr Frazer was something of a Peterhead legend and had, over the years, won the respect of his charges and was regarded as fair, helpful and humane. (The nickname came from the now disgraced and reviled TV star Jimmy Savile and his TV programme.) Frazer gave Walter the unwanted news that Peterhead was his final destination. He was also able to tell Walter a further piece of bad news. His old police adversary from the "High Road" days in Glasgow, detective Joe Beattie, was in hospital. James Frazer was in touch with him regularly by mail and Walter asked that his respects should be passed on to the famous policeman. Norval and Beattie were on different sides of the law, but respected each other. To Norval, Beattie was a fair man doing his job, who did not resort to the fit-up tactics of some dodgy Glasgow cops, one of whom once told me with a straight face that he had never fitted-up anyone who was not guilty. Norval's attitude to Beattie and their degree of mutual respect is not the norm in these more complex days!

Another Peterhead con Walter ran into back in Peterhead was one Joe "The Meek" Meechan who had served time in Polmont Borstal with him. Over a cup of tea they also swapped old stories. There is a strange effect of long-term imprisonment that warps time. When "inside," the monotony and similarity of each day burns the slightest deviation from the norm into the memory. Things that happened years ago are recalled just as if they had happened yesterday. Walter had once given The Meek a jacket and long forgotten the gift. To the old lag it seemed only a short time had passed and he thanked Walter for the kindness. It had apparently been a good quality gift. And the pair of them had a laugh at Joe's disappointment that during his infrequent spells on the outside fate had failed to make him rich, something that Joe had considered inevitable because, as he put it: The Bible makes it clear that The Meek shall inherit the earth!

Relations between prisoners and their guards are extremely varied and in any prison they range from the attitude that Walter adopted – keep your head down and just do the time – to the violent antagonism of others to their captors. Later in this book we will delve into the seriously nasty relationships that soured life in the prison in the 1970s and '80s. But the less desperate incidents of the quieter days of the 1960s and early '70s live on in the memories of such as Willie Leitch, famed as The Saughton Harrier after he ran away from the Edinburgh nick surrounded by marathon runners who were passing the prison. He had popped on a prepared running vest and fake numbered bib, jumped the fence of the governor's garden and joined the athletes.

Walter had been a Category A prisoner in Barlinnie, a man deemed to be more desperate, indeed a menace to society, than the run-of-the-mill con. After his status was reviewed in Peterhead he was assigned to the tailors' shop. Here he was, yet again in a long prison career, in the company of the Saughton Harrier. When these two old lags meet today they still have a good laugh at the prison officer who was visited in the jail by the cops checking out leads in Glasgow's still unsolved 1968 and 1969 Bible John murders. The separate murders of three innocent young women who had gone to Glasgow's famous east end ballroom, Barrowland, which was situated on top of the equally famous Barrows street market, made headlines for almost a year in the Glasgow papers, the douce *Herald* devoting as much space to the search for the killer as the tabloids.

A feature of the case was an early example of the use of identikit posters in the murder hunt. No one who was in Glasgow at the time can forget the striking artist's impression of the killer. It was everywhere on billboards and in the newspapers themselves. The trouble was that the close-cropped red hair and the angular features of the man in the drawing sparked hundreds of comments from the good folk of the city who felt they could recognise the man. He was a Glasgow "type," if there is such a thing. The cops dutifully followed up every lead. Even a totally innocent colleague of mine was stopped at a suburban railway station on his way into work. For days his travelling companions had remarked on his likeness to the poster and eventually made their suspicions known to the police. It was true to say that my newspaper friend did look a *little* like the man in the wanted poster.

His embarrassment was a little less than that of a uniformed Peterhead prison officer interviewed in his own jail by the top brass of Glasgow CID. Boy did that give the Peterhead cons something to talk about over those endless cups of tea. However, the fact is that the officer who was in charge of laundry at that time did, like my colleague, look *a little* like the poster. Do not bet against the notion that the similarity had been pointed out by someone behind bars, maybe even the con who had nicknamed the "screw" Bible John as soon as the papers carrying the Identikit started to appear. Convicts with time on their hands know how to stir things up!

Walter was a serial wrongdoer and a general scourge on society, but he is an intelligent man and his observations of how he ended up back in PH in the 1970s is interesting. A decade earlier he had spent many years there as a result of a typical knife-wielding Glasgow back-court brawl in which he used a chib to such effect that his opponent, one Big Mick Gibson, who had shown a reckless desire to move into Walter's patch, would have died but for some clever work by the guys who use medical scalpels rather than implements that Jim Bowie would have been proud to own. Walter did the crime and did the time, as he says with gangsterish pride. But the confinement, deprivation and general misery he endured on his first visit up north, which lasted for many years, had no beneficial effect on his way of life nor had it installed any fear of a return to the prison fortress in the North-East. On release he went on his usual way – plotting bank robberies one after another. And enjoying spending the proceeds on gambling, good food and drink and holidays in the Spanish sunshine with his attractive blonde mistress, Jean McKinnon. Like many of the robber bankers of today he enjoyed the high life to the full on what might be called ill-gotten gains.

His new one-man crime wave after his release from Peterhead led to a dramatic series of trials in the High Court in Glasgow in the late 1970s. This was a many-faceted affair,

Walter and his connections became known, as the XYY gang since the press, when reporting an interlocking series of crimes had, because of legal problems, been instructed not to identify the several accused till all the trials were over. Instead the symbols X or Y were used by the papers, and only after proceedings were complete were all the names revealed and a legal jigsaw completed. No matter, the sensation that the series of trials caused – the imposing structure of the High Court in Glasgow itself was firebombed in a failed attempt to destroy evidence – left Norval in Barlinnie again in 1977, a Category A prisoner. Officially a "menace to society."

As already noted he was soon to take the road north out of Glasgow back to the North-East. The reason is interesting. As he prowled lonely landings in Barlinnie, his Category A status meant he was denied the companionship of his fellow villains and had to exercise on his own and suffer additional restrictive punishments. He ate his meals by himself in his cell, the door of which was decorated with a large letter A in case anyone in the prison was not aware that here was where one of the hardest of hard tickets laid his head. He certainly had plenty of time to ponder a favourite bee in his bonnet. He had long felt that there was unfairness in the way society seemed, to him, to put a higher value on property and money rather than human life. Was stealing cash more evil than crimes like rape, sexual assault and murder? It looked that way to the Godfather. And this second journey to Peterhead confirmed it to him.

In this instance, in the Bar-L before his second stint in Peterhead, he had, at least, the consolation of sharing the jail with old companions from his previous long stint in the North-East for the attempted murder of Mick Gibson.

He recalls two men in particular, Tony Smith and Billy Fullerton. Fullerton was an offspring of "King Billy" Fullerton who had led the Brigton Billy Boys in sectarian gang rumbles with the Catholic gang the Norman Conks, led by Bull Bowman in the Glasgow of the 1930s. The Billy Boys also had innumerable battles with the Untouchables, the hard-man cops led by the scourge of the Glasgow gangs, Sir Percy Sillitoe. These low-life friends, Tony and Billy, managed, despite Walter's pariah status, to slip the odd morning tabloid under his cell door and even on occasion to arrange an illicit cup of tea. Walter told me that Tony and Billy were, "A hundred per cent genuine cons. The screws would shout at them to get away from my door but the lads would just tell them to fuck off as they were talking to a friend!"

The change in Walter's A category status came about when a visiting dignitary to the prison noticed his exclusion from normal prison life, as he exercised alone, and the VIP took his case up with the authorities. The result was the decision to send him to Peterhead. It was another example of the need for visiting committees and good access to what was going on inside jails for concerned people outside the penal community. The journey north did nothing to disillusion Walter about his theories on the disparity in the treatment of offenders jailed for crimes of violence and sexual misconduct and that of what he considered "old-time" criminals who indulged in thieving and extorting. As he waited in Barlinnie for transfer to the north, Walter was able to mingle with such old lags as Barney Noon from Maryhill and Billy and Vinnie Manson, who had done time with him in Scotland's jails in the past.

But it was not long before an early-morning knock on

107

Walter's cell door informed him that he was to have a wash sharpish and meet the Serious Crime Squad waiting at prison reception to speed him by car to a new place of incarceration. Always a cool customer, he shouted his goodbyes to his mates in the long lines of cells. "I'm going up north, lads," he exclaimed jauntily.

Two cars headed out that cold grey Glasgow morning, both heading north – destination either Perth, Craiginches in Aberdeen or the feared Peterhead. In one car was a man convicted of rape and murder, in the other the infamous bank robber and Godfather. Huddled and huckled in the back seats of the police limos the prisoners saw the River Tay approaching and then disappear in the rear mirrors. Perth was not the destination. This gave Walter the certainty that he was bound for Craiginches rather than the heavy-duty Peterhead. He should have remembered the court appearance when he got fourteen years for bank robbery while a man in a nearby court got seven for killing a three-year-old girl. Had he done so he would not have been so surprised when Jim Frazer, as mentioned earlier, knocked on his dog box that day and told him he was going to Peterhead.

On the last few miles as he watched the rich farmlands speed past, Walter remembered his first approach to PH. Then there was not the comfort of a police limo – he was in a rickety prison bus. As it rattled along, one of the passengers, an old con with the ironic nickname "Sheriff," leaned over and pointed out to the Glaswegians new to the area the prominent local landmark that was the lighthouse on Buchan Ness. On this journey back to the old jail Walter could remember night after night lying abed listening to the Boddam Coo as if it was yesterday. It was not a pleasant memory. The nearness of the huge red-and-white-striped tower of the lighthouse was a wake-up call to the fact that soon the huge gates of PH would swing open, the car would drive through, and the gates swing shut with a thud that said goodbye to freedom.

Throughout his long prison life Walter Norval eschewed any forelock touching or overdone deference to authority. That was not his style. He liked to be called Wattie and he called governors or warders alike by their first names, he was Wattie, they were Sam or Agnes or whatever. It was a technique that made him memorable inside. He retained this informality for this new incarceration. He found the prison routine little changed from his previous visit. Each morning the cons assembled in the main yard and were marched down what they called "The Burma Road" to the work sheds. The Category A men never left the yard till the others were away and they were last up at lunch and teatime. They were searched on leaving the main hall and when they entered and left the yard. And again on entering and leaving their work shed. On average they were searched eight times a day. Telling me this over a coffee Walter remarked wryly and accurately, "I don't think they trusted us."

The layman, knowing that many of these cons had the skill to control large numbers of men and carefully plot and plan bank raids, might be forgiven for thinking such a regime of search after search was, maybe, just a wise precaution, especially in a prison where the cons had a tendency to use improvised weapons against officers or to take any opportunity they could to break out on to the roof to spend a happy hour or two throwing slates at their captors. Or maybe even making an attempt to burn the place down.

Once a Godfather always a Godfather and Walter found his sage advice much in demand in his second stint. He admired the attitude of one of the youngsters who asked for his help. John Steele, or "Johnnyboy" as they called him, had a happy-go-lucky style about him. Walter says, "You would have thought it was twelve hours not twelve years he was facing." Mind you, prison officers of the time remember young Steele as a handful. Most of the hard tickets in Peterhead at that time had no compassion for their victims, no concern for those they had hurt. Remorse was not in plentiful supply.

But there is the exception, and even the toughest of the tough can have a compassionate side. At one stage of his second Peterhead stay a visitor happened to show Walter a picture of a baby dying of kidney disease in Glasgow's internationally renowned Yorkhill children's hospital. The Godfather showed the touching snap to some fellow cons and they decided to do something to help the hospital. At that time wee woolly rabbits and floppy big-eared elephants and soft toys of any kind were not normally found in Peterhead. But the cons used prison wages to buy material and set about the unlikely task of making some. It must have been a bizarre sight – the hard tickets surrounded by felt and stuffing, working at creating toys for the Yorkhill kids. Walter's mistress, Jean McKinnon, along with the grandmother of the baby in the photograph headed north on a visit and returned home with sacks of soft toys for distribution in the wards of the great hospital on the banks of the Clyde. It certainly gives a different impression of the hard men locked up in Peterhead.

Letters from home were particularly important to prisoners fifty or sixty years ago before mobiles and emails, and especially in a place like Peterhead many miles from the slums of Glasgow. Jean McKinnon was a leggy eye-catcher with some style, a real looker, as they say. But she found time to be a diligent letter writer, penning a note every day or so to her "man" held up north. She seldom missed a day and took every opportunity to visit him, an arduous journey especially in the winter. But Walter still paid the bills for his wife Ina and sent Christmas gifts and other "wee mindings" to her on a regular basis. Cash was sent by his handlers, as he called them, on the outside, for a wee break at Glasgow Fair. And the kids got their Easter eggs and birthday cards.

Having two women in his life was no problem to Walter, always a bit of a ladies' man. But the arrangement on occasion caused some laughter in the prison among the warders. Walter remembers the day Jean turned up a few hours after Ina had made a visit. The warder, trying hard to keep a straight face, told him, "Your wife is here to see you. And this one is a blonde!"

But relations between the screws and cons could also be edgy. Many of the screws arrived at work with neat packages of sandwiches or other morsels to see them through a tough day of supervising the awkward squad of cons. One particular day Norval and his pals noticed that one guy, instead of the usual gammon on white or whatever, had brought in a couple of duck eggs. He had bought them as a treat before going on shift as his wife had not had the time to make up the sannies that day. When the screw went about his business Walter slipped into the kitchen and nicked a couple of hen eggs, which he used to promptly replace the duck ones, which he was partial to. The screw's eggs boiled and eaten, the cons had a lot of fun listening to the officer and his pals trying to find out what had happened to miraculously change the nature of his much-looked-forward-to little treat. It was an unsolved mystery that helped pass the time for the crims and their keepers for many an hour.

This sentence was a long haul for Norval. And after two and a half years, not long if you say it quickly, there was still years to wait till his feet again walked the pavements of Possilpark. But at this point there was a welcomed improvement in his conditions – his security status was reassessed and he was allowed to take a cushy job in the storeroom. He acknowledged the irony of a one-time armed bank robber now spending his life behind a counter, for all the world like a shopkeeper. It was, too, a change to be one of the "good lads" behind bars rather than a feared outsider. Now he had a bit more freedom to move around the jail and a bit of responsibility. On a monthly basis he ordered clothing and stores and decided what material needed replacing.

This job helped him work out the remaining long years of his time in Peterhead in a relatively quiet life with the most taxing questions being who to leave in and out of his hall's football team. Always a leader, this remarkable criminal was a success on the sports field. When it was coming close to the time his sentence would be over he was transferred south to Dungavel prison near Strathaven in Lanarkshire to complete his sentence. At last the gates were opened for him. He was free to go back on to the streets of Glasgow. He had served his time up north and "escaped" legally. Unlike a man he knew well in the prison, a certain Gentle Johnny Ramensky.

8

MORE GUNS, FEAR ON THE STREETS
AND NASTY SOUP

Guards, jailers, warders, prison officers – those whose task it is to keep violent and dangerous men locked away and to make sure they pose no danger to the public – have down the years had a succession of names and name changes. The preferred description these days is "prison officer" and much of their training has changed from the old days when they were "jailors." The job in the twenty-first century entails more than just making sure the cell doors are locked. Training for release is an important part of the job – as is the difficult task of tackling the problem of reoffending. The training and educational standards are high. But it can still be a dangerous occupation, as the wife of one Peterhead prison officer told me: "You are always prepared for the worst, hostage taking, physical attacks and such like." It is a pleasant moment when your husband turns up back at the front door safe and sound after yet another demanding shift working with the hard men who are caged in a top-security jail. Mind you, there can on occasion be a touch of humour and this lady laughed as she remembered her man coming home, his shirt and uniform slashed with red – but it was not blood, simply beetroot juice poured over him at mealtime by a disgruntled con!

Incidents are not always so harmless. Folk on the outside are generally unaware how the odds can stack up against an officer. The daily routine has officers moving large groups of prisoners to exercise in the yards or to work in places like the tailors' shop or the quarry in the case of Peterhead and, of course, the officers are heavily outnumbered and immediately in difficulties if a large group gangs up on them. Hence the fact that in the early days, guns and cutlasses were a vital part of the uniform, as has been noted. The shooting in the quarry before the Second World War demonstrated that. But even as late as 1959 some officers had rifles at hand and one told me of a dangerous incident with a work party in the Admiralty yard.

The cons, around forty of them, were at work making concrete blocks. At each end of the work line an officer stood with his weapon at the ready. Normally there was no trouble, as the majority of the prisoners were conditioned to respond to officers' orders and move around as directed without much fuss. The conditioning, of course, coming from years of following a rigid routine. But you cannot always be completely sure that the men you are supervising will be docile and compliant.

This day prisoners were using spades – always a potentially dangerous weapon – as they went about their work. One guy, presumably nursing a grievance, suddenly lifted his spade to threaten an officer and the other officer responded with a shot in textbook fashion. The training was always to shoot to disable rather than kill and the shoulders were a preferred target. This guy neatly sent a bullet into the arm of the threatening prisoner. It was a nice piece of sharp-shooting, but the bullet ricocheted around the concrete blocks and there was much ducking and diving. Clean underwear was needed for both prisoners and guards. Shortly after this incident the guns were finally removed from prison officers, despite in this case preventing a dangerous attack.

This incident carries a curious echo with an incident reported away back in the early years of the prison in 1896. No shots were fired in this case, which was reported under the heading of "OUTBREAK AT PETERHEAD CONVICT PRISON – Mutinous Attack On Warders." The news had just leaked out, said the paper, and it said: "It appears that over half a dozen prisoners had been employed in a cement shed shovelling material when one of them rebelled against the orders of a warder. The dissatisfaction spread to the whole gang and it is asserted that shovels were flung freely by the convicts, a warder being severely hurt on his ankles and one of his feet. Thereupon the warders drew their swords – one of them a six-foot retired Life Guardsman having his sword at 'the draw' stating very placidly, but firmly, that if the convicts did not recommence work at once he would assuredly cut down the first one he got at. One of the convicts was then handcuffed with his hands behind his back and in the presence of Mr McGhee, the head warder, inclined to be obstreperous when the officer knocked him flat on his back. The convict kicked out with his feet but was ultimately quietened and work resumed." All in a day's work in Peterhead!

All prison officers have anecdotes of such incidents, happenings that they will never forget. They may not get talked about much in public, as those in the prison service tend to be discreet, but they are always there, deep in the psyche. A veteran prison officer, Bert Whyte, an Aberdeen-shire man now in his late seventies, ended up as an executive at the women's prison Cornton Vale near Stirling. His early days were a bit more exciting and dangerous than that particular spell of duty. He tells an intriguing story of the night he could have been kidnapped or even murdered.

Bert first came to Peterhead after working as an electrical engineer in the RAF. A man with his skills is always in demand in a prison – keeping the alarms, floodlights, and telecommunications instruments and suchlike in order is similar to maintaining the Forth Rail Bridge – no sooner is one snag fixed than another comes along demanding attention. Particularly in a place like Peterhead, built in the 1880s and altered and brought up to modern standards over the years, or as near as possible given the design of the place. The North Sea wind and sea air also took a heavy toll on electrical equipment.

After Bert has spent some time working in the prison as an outside contractor his wife, Ellen, still an elegant and alert woman, thought that it might be a good idea for her husband to have a chat with her uncle. This gentleman was in the prison service and he was persuasive when he explained to his young relative why a job in the service might be worthwhile. There was job security, a decent wage, a house, a chance to still use some of his engineering skills and to put something back into society helping rehabilitate some who had gone astray. That is if the prisoner had the will to reform. If rehabilitation was out of the question, as was often the case with the hard tickets selected to do their time in Peterhead, the prison service was still of great value to the public making sure villains could do no more harm.

That protection of the public was, and is, a vital aim of the

116

service. Ellen Whyte herself knew this well, as she remembered the feeling of fear and apprehension she felt as a teenager when the good folk of Peterhead heard the warning
sound of the prison bell ringing out loudly announcing
someone or other had absconded or escaped. The local
radio, too, would cover any breakout in some depth,
warning of the danger from desperate men on the run. She
told me what it was like when one of the "connies," as she
and her young pals called them, was on the loose outside
the grim walls. On nights like that there were no trips into
town for an hour or two at the dancing or the cinema and
every moving shadow or echoing footstep was a worry.

Peterhead's young girls could develop a crick in the
neck. So she knew well the dangers the officers faced. But,
of course, you got on with life. A highlight of their early
married life was when Bert bought his first car – a second-
hand Ford Consul that he was immensely proud to own. He
kept it in wooden huts near the prison in the Admiralty yard,
a once bustling place but by then used mainly for storage.
As a concession some of the officers were allowed to garage
their cars there. So one wintry night Bert found himself
listening to howling wind and rain but was happy working
on his Ford in the shelter of the shed. Cars in these days
seemed covered in acres of unnecessary chrome. Owners
bought tubes of chrome cleaner by the dozen and spent
hours with yellow polishing clothes getting the car to gleam
and removing flecks of rust. One night he was enjoying
himself at this task under the light of a lamp rigged up using
the car battery, after all he was an electrical engineer, when
he for no clear reason felt there was someone else nearby.
He stopped and took a look, uneasy but not sure why. He
heard banging noises but saw nothing, so he finished the

polishing and decided to head back to the prison, stopping on the way for a pint with mates in a little recreation club for officers.

Right away he knew something was wrong and as they sipped their beers his pals told him that three bad 'uns were on the run. Apparently a farm gate that was opened to let a prison van into the Admiralty yard had been accidently left open and the cons had purloined another van and driven into the yard. Hence the banging noises! Bert was summoned to the governor's office, where the boss told him what had happened, but in the darkness Bert had seen nothing useful to help the hunt for the cons who were in any case soon recaptured. But that led to an interesting confrontation in the prison some time later. One of the escapers that night was John "Gypsy" Winning, a notorious Glasgow low-lifer who was involved in the Paddy Meehan saga told elsewhere in this book. Another player in this tale of wrongful conviction was the infamous Glasgow criminal William "Tank" McGuiness, who was himself murdered in a street brawl.

The last person to see him alive was Winning, who was charged with his murder but the case collapsed because of insufficient evidence. Clearly Winning was not a man to be tangled with lightly. Not long after his recapture on this occasion he ran into Bert Whyte in the prison. Winning said to Bert, "You are a very lucky man," as he could have caught the escapers in a shed near the one where he garaged his car. Bert said he thought he was never near the escapers but Winning told him that he had been within a few yards of them and they had decided if he had spotted them to thump him and then tape him up and throw him into the van they were using to get away from the prison. This van was eventually found deep down at the bottom of a quarry

118

at Inverurie. Bert has ever since wondered if he had challenged the escapers would he have been found dead inside that abandoned van? Would the men on the run have taken the trouble to free him before driving the van into the deep hole to hide it? The record of John "Gypsy" Winning indicates that it was unlikely. Bert had indeed a lucky escape.

Winning also features in another nasty story of life in Peterhead told by Bert Whyte. It might have been called the Cat Man of Peterhead, a sort of reversal of the Bird Man of Alcatraz. Ironically such a title would have been more accurate than the famous film was – for Robert Stroud, the bird man of the title, kept his birds in Leavenworth Penitentiary not Alcatraz. When he moved to the famous island in San Francisco Bay he was not allowed to keep pets. But Hollywood, like many a newspaper man, did not like letting the facts spoil a good story.

Winning did not have official approval to keep pets but he had somehow made friends with a local feral cat who accessed his cell via a window and spent time with the con. Cats, it seems, take people as they find them and are no respecters of reputations. Winning was not popular with prison officers or most of his fellow cons. Perhaps his only real friend in life was that cat.

Some of the cons decided to wreak revenge on Winning. He was part of a little group who had access to boiling water to make their own tea and sandwiches. One evening when Winning was returned to his cell after being in a work party his mates asked if he fancied a plate of soup. The cons watched this evil man sup it with some keen interest. Afterwards they asked if he had enjoyed it. The answer was in the affirmative. They then told him the main ingredient had been his cat. "Gypsy" Winning went berserk at the news and had to be restrained. Indeed it was weeks before his fearful anger against his fellow cons subsided. Life in a prison can take bizarre and unpleasant turns and most cons take care that no one urinates in their tea or other similar nastiness. But cat soup – that was a notch above anything even the most suspicious would expect.

The prison population in Scotland is constantly shifting as villains are shuffled from one place of incarceration to another. Repeat offenders tend to be familiar with all the old jails, in particular Saughton, Barlinnie, Peterhead and Perth. And in each they tend to renew old friendships made during long spells inside. One such was John "Mad Dog" Duggan who had an infamous reputation in Peterhead after making something of a name for himself as an escaper or potential escaper in the '60s and '70s. The main break that made his name among the cons and put him on to the tabloid front pages was from Barlinnie not Peterhead. But it is worth recounting in order to illustrate the daring and ingenuity of the men who managed to get over the walls of Scotland's prisons.

Duggan was in the untried prisoner section when he made his plans. But not everyone sharing porridge with him was a friend. A fellow prisoner tipped the word of the imminent escape attempt to Les Brown, a legendary detective who rose to the top of the CID in Glasgow and a man with possibly the best contact book of informers in gangland then or now. Les was a tall, powerful figure but his ear was metaphorically always on the ground. Little happened in the underworld that he did not hear about. Tipped off on Mad Dog's intentions he naturally told the then Bar-L governor, but Mr Mackenzie, a generally respected and efficient boss of the tough establishment who had also ruled

An evocative early picture of the Harbour of Refuge under construction showing the prison as it looked in the early days of the last century. The huge south breakwater edges slowly out into the North Sea, but it was more than 50 years till the humanitarian project was finally complete.

An impressive demonstration of why the Peterhead breakwaters, among the largest in the world, were needed so that vessels could shelter and sit out the violent storms. Huge seas pound the stonework put in place by convict labour.

A drawing illustrating the hard labour that was used in the quarries in the early days. Back then muscle power was king.

Gentle Johnny Ramensky, a Lithuanian safe cracker and war-time Commando hero in the British Army, wrote himself into the criminal history of Scotland as the greatest jail escaper ever. In this front page he shows weariness and physical decline.

Oscar Slater, fitted up by the establishment in Glasgow for a murder he did not commit, is a name forever linked with Peterhead. Sentenced to hang in 1909, he was reprieved but not released until 1927 after much public campaigning.

Walter Norval kept a cocky smile on his face as he left court after being sentenced to long years in Peterhead. He was Glasgow's first Godfather, a bank robber and meticulous criminal planner.

T.C. Campbell was a Glasgow hard man who ended up in Peterhead for a crime he had no part in – the Glasgow Ice Cream Wars murders. He and his co-accused, Joe Steele, constantly pleaded their innocence. Campbell and Steele had their convictions quashed – after twenty years!

As Peterhead waits for the bulldozers and the new HMP Grampian nears completion next door, care is being taken to preserve as much of the history of the old prison as is possible. Out from dusty cupboards and forgotten corners have emerged some remarkable photographs and pieces of memorabilia. The evocative prison railway scenes are among the most striking images in this montage, as is the cat o' nine tails.

The Staff housing seen here was in two tenements of 18 flats and 36 flats. The black gable-ended structure visible in this photo at the end of '18 quarter' was the staff club, a corrugated iron structure.

THE CAT O'NINE TAILS

The cat should weigh 9 ounces, comprised of a covered wooden handle 19½ inches long with nine lashes of whipcord. Each lash of approx. one eighth of an inch thick, and 33 inches long, tipped with cat. Only those over 21 could be lashed. There was no upper age limit. Abolished in the Criminal Justice (Scotland) Act 1949.

STAFF OF THE MID 1920's.

To burn a prison down is too often, around the world, an ambition of desperate men held behind bars. Rooftop protests also are something of a norm in prison riots. Peterhead has had plenty of both. This shot shows the ferocity of the blaze during the riot of 1986.

Hostage taking is another evil ploy of caged and violent men wanting to make a protest. Here in the riots of 1987 – quelled eventually by unprecedented action by the SAS – prison officer Jackie Stuart is paraded on the roof at the end of a rope, his life in danger. Jackie survived to become a Peterhead prison legend.

Paddy Meehan was a small-time safebreaker and burglar wrongly convicted of murder in 1969 and sent to Peterhead. There he spent long years in solitary, always pleading his innocence and always at war with the prison authorities. He received a free pardon in 1976.

One infamous name carved into the violent history of the prison is Jimmy Boyle. A cruel player in Glasgow's gangland, he served many years in Peterhead before he was transferred to the controversial Barlinnie Special Unit. But "up north" he is remembered as a dangerous and violent man far removed from this smiling image.

Inside the prison in its later days with echoing corridors, institutional white paint and officers always at the ready in case of attack from cons with a grievance. But beneath the walkways are pool tables. Chronic lack of space meant no real recreation areas.

The new prison is impressive in this view, though it has none of the scary grimness of the old Peterhead. Hopefully the regime inside will be more concentrated on rehabilitation than revenge. Those who criticise the lack of obvious signs of bars to cage the prisoners might reflect that the old jail, however tough, was never short of return clients.

Peterhead for some years, had more faith in his prison's security than Duggan and took no action. The tip-off was noted but Mackenzie was not losing sleep over it. Not much later it was Les Brown who had his sleep disturbed by a 3am phone call asking him to contact the prison. It transpired that Duggan had somehow removed the bars from his cell window and climbed out onto the roof. His next move was to swing hand over hand on telephone wires to get on to the gatehouse roof. He had "booked" a getaway car to meet him. But on jumping onto the ground outside the prison he got a shock. He was on his own in the dark. No prison warders at his heels, no screaming alarm bells in his ears. But no getaway car either. His erstwhile helper had given him, as they say in Glasgow, a "dizzy." There was nothing to do but leg it away into the silent streets surrounding the prison. Mr Mackenzie may not have heeded the tip-off but now he wanted Les Brown's help in getting his guest back.

After a week when Duggan lay low in Possilpark, as much a prisoner as he had been in the Bar-L, freedom seemed a less attractive proposition and he got his wife to phone big Les, who promptly turned up in the Duggan home with a colleague, detective sergeant Jim Montgomery. All three tucked into bacon and eggs before setting out to take the escaper back to Barlinnie. But that was only temporary – Duggan duly went to court and was convicted and soon on his way to Peterhead for a longer stay.

Les forgot about Duggan till much later when he got an amusing reminder of him from reports in the tabloids. Peterhead was by then the focus of numerous riots, rooftop protests and all sorts of mayhem. Les almost choked on a chocolate digestive when he saw a picture of the latest protest – there was Mad Dog Duggan on the roof of

Peterhead holding a placard reading: FUCK NELSON MANDELA – FREE ME.

There might have been a touch of unconscious humour here, for Les still laughs when he recalls some high jinks when Duggan was originally arrested. He had used a tad too much "jelly" in a raid on the Scottish Gas office in Sauchiehall Street, Glasgow, and the target safe was blown out onto the street. When the cops arrived they were told that the safe-blower had been seen on the roof of the nearby Apollo Theatre – now gone, but then a legendary venue for pop and rock shows. The building was surrounded and searched but that night it had been booked for an Asian community film show. The audience were mostly in turbans and in a vain attempt to hide himself, Duggan had tried to make one from his T-shirt. The bright spark asked the cops who collared him, "How did you recognise me?" Les and his fellow boys in blue were too busy laughing to explain. Duggan, it seems, also had a sense of humour when in Peterhead. Even on the rooftop!

9

RAB THE CAT, CEMENT HEID
AND SEAGULLS GALORE

The antics of such as Walter Norval and Mad Dog Duggan in displaying a sense of humour behind bars are not unique. Prisoners with time on their hands and a lively brain can find ways to inject a laugh or two into the bleak days of prison routine. And no one could do it better than one long-time inhabitant of Peterhead, James Crosbie, inevitably nicknamed Bing by his pals, but in his day known to the tabloids as "Britain's most wanted man." Some years ago he published his amusing story of his years in Peterhead.

In 1974 Crosbie was a successful businessman with an enviable lifestyle. But he was bored and turned to armed robbery. A somewhat dramatic cure for something we all suffer from from time to time. He was so bored indeed that he relieved one bank of around £70,000 without taking the trouble to exchange a few pleasantries with a teller or write a withdrawal slip. This resulted in a different sort of boredom. Prison boredom required to be fought with a maximum sense of humour and making the most of any chance for a laugh. Crosbie's memoir *Peterhead Porridge* is extremely funny but also tinged with some significant sadness and it gives an insight into day-to-day prison life in a way few other books have. Well worth a read.

And in amongst the laughs he makes some serious and sometimes surprising observations. He will tell you that prisoners facing long sentences can sometimes come to terms with doing the time easier than those "only" in for a year or so. The reason is that the guy on the shorter tariff counts every day, almost every hour. If you are facing a decade or so behind bars that sort of thinking is pointless. There is no light at the end of the tunnel, only darkness stretching far into the future. In such circumstances counting the days only ratchets up the pain of confinement – instead you take each day as it comes, any future outside of the bars is virtually non-existent. So you try not to let it trouble you.

And part of the technique to maximise prison humour is to use nicknames. Being reduced to a prison number (181-74 in Crosbie's case) can be numbing and in prison, as in factories and other places with repetitive routines, nicknames add a certain colour to daily life. In the 1970s Peterhead had a full share of characters and some mad nicknames, for prisoners and "screws" alike. Take the cons, for a start. They included Rent A Rope, Batman, Raving Rampton Rab, Bald Eagle, the Saughton Harrier (our old friend Willie Leitch), Sodjer Thompson, Flame On, Davie Doughnut, the Mad Major, Rab the Cat, Stinky Steve, Gentle Johnny (Ramensky), Big Nellie and the Godfather himself (Walter Norval). Big Nellie acquired his nickname, as it is not too hard to guess, from his obvious sexual orientation. And it is said that on occasion in the exercise yard he was taunted by the more macho cons on his predilection for same-sex sex. He used to deal with this in contemptuous fashion by shouting back at his tormentors, "Aye and I've had him, him and him pointing out the cons he meant to all and sundry." It was a successful ploy.

Nellie was for a long time the prison bookmaker. Most cons like a gamble and the racing papers are at a premium and the punters have a lot of time on their hands to study form. The currency for behind-bars gambling was, of course, tobacco which could be bought in small quantities. Nellie ran the book and paid out when required. But it was not a good idea to run up too much debt. If you had not enough baccy to pay what you owed, Nellie would decide to ignore the debt in return for a sexual favour or two.

Incidentally, tobacco smoothed some of rough edges of prison life in other ways. A good prison officer always had an ear to what was going on, keeping track of what prison feuds were brewing and the formation of different and antagonistic "teams" among the prisoners. You needed inside info on that in order to take early action to put a stop to any little wars that were boiling under the surface. And one way to get it was to drop a little baccy into the right palms. Care was required and officers and cons were adept at the transfer of the inducement from warder to con. In a line of cons with their back to their captors an open hand might be slipped behind a con's back and the baccy dropped into it unnoticed. No chances were taken, as it was not a good idea for a con to be known as being in the pocket of an officer and grassing on fellow prisoners. Identification as a grass or toady to the officers would lead to verbal and physical abuse from the cons who hated their jailers.

The officers were given equally eccentric monikers – Fairy Queen, Banana Back, Bible John, Cement Heid, Hank the Yank, Gibbering Gibby, Red Alert, Deputy Dawg, Hess

(Jackie Stuart, who was to be taken hostage in one of the major riots of the late '80s), Jelly Buttocks and The Gimp. Even in 2013, in the final months of the prison, nicknames were rife. I spoke to one senior officer enquiring awkwardly if he, too, had a moniker.

He smiled and said, "Of course, we all have."

It was a clear invitation to ask, "What was yours?"

He smiled back and said, "Surely you can guess?"

"No," I said, letting down the school of thought that thinks all journos are trained observers.

"Well it is Wing Nuts."

Why on earth . . . ?

"Take a good look," he said, then I belatedly got it – this officer had ears rather on the large side!

The old nicknames all feature when Bing talks of his prison life. Earlier in this book the fate of Gypsy Winning's cat was told. Winning was not the only con with a pet of sorts. Crosbie notes that keeping pigeons was something of a prison hobby that had a bit of a blind eye turned on it by the prison authorities, who no doubt thought that feeding the odd crumb to a bird on the ledge outside your cell was harmless. Indeed it might even have a calming effect on the men in such a high-security prison.

One of the aforementioned prison guards was called Cement Heid, this sobriquet coming from the fact that before joining the prison service he used to drive a lorry delivering cement to the prison. In this occupation he noticed that the warders led what to him seemed a cushy life. So he parked the lorry and applied to join the prison service. The nickname could also have had something to do with the fact that the cons did not consider him an ideal candidate for *Brain of Britain* on the radio. Or indeed any quiz show.

The aptness of this judgement could be seen in the story of Cement Heid and the pigeons. The guard had taken against a particular prisoner and had decided as a punishment to remove his pet birds. This he proposed to do by throwing them out of the window, seemingly unaware of the homing habits of such creatures. A fellow officer remonstrated with Cement Heid and said there was only one way to get rid of such a bird, demonstrating by picking up the unfortunate nearest pigeon and ringing its neck in front of its owner.

As in the case of Winning's cat, this became a cause célèbre in the prison and although the owner had wisely kept his hands to himself at the time of the assassination, a letter arrived at the Royal Society of Protection of Birds. Bing and his pals waited for retribution for the bird killer. Some hope – the Society said pigeons were vermin and the method of disposal had been humane!

What is it about birds and prisoners? Apart from the Peterhead pigeons the skies around the old penitentiary were full of seagulls. These handsome wild birds were on the edge of their more normal habitat – seashore. But, of course, they soon twigged that there were easy pickings around the jail and sat on the rooftops watching for a prisoner to drop a crumb or two before swooping down. An old dodge that gave veterans a laugh was to get a newly arrived prisoner to cross the yard with a tray of bread which soon created a scene worthy of Hitchcock, as the wild birds dive-bombed the victim in search of a free meal.

It is never a good idea to confide any fears you have to fellow cons – any weakness is exploited as soon as it is admitted. Joe Polding – nicknamed the Mallet – had been a henchman of Glasgow Godfather Walter Norval in his bank robbing days and was as tough as they come. But this hard

127

man from the Glasgow streets was afraid of the gulls. This caught the attention of one of the prison's practical jokers. One night this guy put out some tempting bread for a gull and when it landed on his window ledge he promptly snared it with a loop of string and stuffed it into a pillow-case. He then waited till the Mallet was out of his cell and hid it in a cupboard. The joker had figured that alone in the dark the frightened bird would sit quietly, which it did. But at lock-up time the bird sensing the quiet falling over the prison became restive. Polding at first put the strange noises down to the wind or wood creaking but after a while he had to investigate. He opened the cupboard door and a huge seagull with a five-foot wingspan flew into his face. The screams could have been heard in Aberdeen. Quite a laugh for Joe's fellow prisoners, though.

A compulsion to seek the company of animals seemed to affect some prisoners. Mice, cats and birds could all be befriended by a con. Maybe they just wanted a quiet listener to their tales of woe and injustice. But others were afraid of insects or wee furry creatures. The infamous Arthur Thompson Snr, who succeeded Walter Norval as Glasgow's Godfather, was remembered for a prison ploy. He noted that a cell near to his was inhabited by a hard man with a weakness. This guy would fight in the streets like a tiger, afraid of no man. But mice? That was another story. Big Arthur decided to have a bit of fun. He managed to get a fragment of brush tied to a bit of string into a pipe in the cell of the man who was scared of mice and pulled the string, producing the most realistic of mice-scratching sounds that drove the con into total distraction.

It would be sad and wrong if "Bing" Crosbie's prison memoirs left the reader with any sort of impression that doing time in Peterhead – or even working there was some kind of fun. Hard men like to play the hard man even when in jail but a few laughs – however entertainingly told – should not be allowed to dilute to any great extent the misery of the place. The shocking fact is that Bing is an intelligent and literate man, if criminal, but spent years in the company of people who were so mentally ill that without a doubt they should have been in a mental hospital rather than a prison. It is ironic that in its final years Peterhead became a specialist place for sex offenders and killers with mental health issues.

The story of one nicknamed offender, Rab the Cat, shows how desperate some of the inmates were. This man, Robert Meechan, was not given his sobriquet in response to skill as a burglar. The "Cat" referred to was the cat o' nine tails. He was the last man in Peterhead to be whipped by this horrific weapon.

How he earned this punishment gives us a remarkable insight into prison life around half a century ago. Meechan had attacked an officer and languished in the prison punishment block, where he was becoming demented because it was a tobacco-free zone. He devised, as they say, a cunning plan. He asked permission to join the prison Sunday bible class. This is the sort of move that delights and enthuses all governors and he got his way. The large attendances at such prison events are often caused by a desire on the behalf of the con to break the boredom of prison rather than take a step towards the religious life. The plan hatched by Rab the Cat was this: he knew the organist smoked a pipe and would have a tobacco pouch on his person and this was his target. He picked his moment to "embrace" the organist, congratulating him on a nifty bit of keyboard work all the while searching for the pouch which he found and snatched from the terrified musician in skilled pickpocket manner. Rab was immediately thrown to the ground by the screws and a wild struggle began. But the Cat would not release the pouch. In the end, however strange as it sounds, a compromise was reached and he was allowed to keep the tobacco if he handed back the pouch. This was done and the governor compensated the organist for his lost tobacco. Mind you, the musician decided that was the end of his career as organist in the jail and he never returned.

For his "assault" on the prison visitor Rab the Cat was sentenced to twenty lashes of the cat o' nine tails. This was the maximum number permitted at the time. Shortly after his ordeal the use of the lash was banned. This gave Rab both his nickname and a place in penal history. He was stretched on a brass frame in the bathhouse to allow the administration of the lashes. For many a year afterwards, prisoners would look at the brass mountings for the frame on which he was stretched, which had never been removed, and thank their lucky stars that they had never suffered in the way Rab the Cat did. But Meechan was one tough con and after his lashing he jumped to his feet and declared, "Give me a couple more fags and I will take the same again." The prison records to be seen to this day grudgingly give acknowledgement of his fortitude in the face of what was, in effect, torture. They note "that he was a man of stout character." Something of an understatement, you might say. His experience did not turn him into a model prisoner. Serving another sentence later in an English prison he again assaulted an officer and was given another touch of the "cat," which was then still in use down south.

The Peterhead cat is still in amongst the collected memorabilia stored in the prison. It is a fearsome weapon and when you look at it you wonder how someone like Meechan could have taken it and asked for more. Around two-and-a-half-feet long it was designed to break the flesh and draw blood. For flogging or whipping you could not find a better weapon, though it would be no fun to be birched either. One touch of the cat should have been enough to deter the worst of criminals. Or so you would think. Incidentally the existing cat held in the prison is in pristine condition. Someone must have wiped it clean of blood and lovingly prepared it for the next victim. The cat could only be used with the express permission of the governor and had to have government approval. It disappeared from the Scottish prison scene in the late 1940s, though in Australia it was in use some years afterwards.

The nickname habit was not restricted to Peterhead or indeed any other jail and while many of the sobriquets were applied to cons or warders low in the pecking order, there was another exclusive tribe – the governors. And nicknames were popular, too, even in Alcatraz, perhaps the most famous penal establishment in the world. The first governor there was James A. Johnstone, known as "Saltwater" for his habit of getting unruly convicts washed down with hoses of sea water. In Alcatraz Governor Swope was "Cowboy" because of his favoured style in hats and another ruler of that hard jail was "Promising Paul" Madigan, who was good at listening to the cons' complaints and promising action but nothing much ever happened despite his constant assurances.

Here in Scotland the governors of Peterhead, Barlinnie, Saughton and Perth and some others often had nicknames, mostly unrepeatable. But one man stands out from the rest – "Slasher" Gallagher, who was Peterhead governor from 1976 to 1979. He was doubly distinguished in the nicknames game because he had two. He was originally "Square Go" Gallagher, so called because he was not adverse to a gloved battle or two in the boxing rings which at one time were a feature of gyms in old prisons and borstals. It was a useful moniker to have in a place where violence bred violence and where you needed to show toughness to gain respect.

In *Peterhead Porridge* James Crosbie gives his version of the re-christening of Governor Gallagher. It is, however, a story that takes "a bit of believing," as he puts it himself. According to the tale, a prisoner had been some months in the protection cells as a precaution after an altercation with another con. Now he was fearful of being placed back on the regular cell blocks where his enemy still strutted around. He was scared of retaliation and came up with an idea that might save him from his fate. He would do something desperate to prolong his stay in the protection cells where he was safe from the other cons. Governor Gallagher had a bit of a routine, like most other governors, of popping into various cells and asking "any complaints" of the inmates. Mind you, this is often a cosmetic PR exercise and in Gallagher's case, and I suspect that of most other governors, you had to be quick with a complaint before a door slammed in your face.

The scared con knew he had to act fast and had with typical cunning prepared well. He melted the head of a toothbrush and inserted a razor blade into it, making a dangerous little weapon. He had got himself all psyched up to use it and when one morning the gov stepped in with his usual "any complaints" routine, he bound forward and lashed out with his makeshift blade, nicking his visitor in the face. The handmade chib dropped to the floor and according to legend, "Square Go" picked it up and replied in kind, drawing blood from his attacker in his anger. The nick on the governor's face was trivial and only required a touch of sticking plaster. It is not mentioned how badly the attacker was injured but the supposition is that it, too, was trivial. This was no Glasgow razor slashing involving much flow of blood and stitching of disfiguring wounds. But any attack on a prisoner could have serious consequences if reported. The escorts of the governor did not put in "a paper" which would have triggered an inquiry, instead a swift deal to water down the whole incident was agreed all round. Mr Gallagher's attacker was soon afterwards on his way to Barlinnie, out of reach of the cons he feared, and the governor gained a new nickname, one that would earn respect in any prison. It also provided an amusing moment for the press when during the infamous Barlinnie siege early in 1987 a banner saying "SLASHER MUST GO" was displayed from the rooftop as slates were hurled down at the warders below. "Who is this guy 'Slasher' and what is he in for?" asked one young newspaperman of a more experienced colleague. He was taken aback to be told that the man in question was not a prisoner but the governor!

Not long after this historic siege ended – it lasted longer than any other in Scottish prison history – there was another amusing incident involving "Slasher." When things had got back to relative normality and the urge for violence no longer flowed so furiously in the blood of the convicts there was a little concert in the prison church hall. Governor Gallagher was present. Every eye in the audience was on him as in one comedy skit a convict/actor appeared thinly disguised as "Slasher." What would be his reaction? The wise old governor broke into a laugh and within seconds the audience joined in! It was a reminder how volatile and changeable emotions in a prison can be.

10

BALACLAVAS, STUN GRENADES
AND THE END OF A RIOT

Two of the most turbulent years in the prison's history were 1986 and 1987. Violent riots both involving the taking of a prison officer hostage occurred one after another, and the story of the second and most infamous of these incidents proved that not all of the problems exposed earlier when the rioters were taken to court had been sorted out. Both riots were milestones in Scottish prison history, events of huge significance and public concern. The fact that such violence had broken out again so soon after the shocking violence of the first riot made the second of the two events even more significant. Who would have thought after the first riot had finally been quelled that not too many months later there would be another violent incident and that for the first time in Scotland the army would be called in to deal with it.

Ask almost anyone of a certain age in Britain what they know about the SAS (Special Air Service) and they will recall some of the most dramatic pictures ever seen on live television – the storming of the Iranian embassy in London in 1980. No one who saw them will ever forget the scenes in broad daylight on a day in May at Princes Gate in South Kensington. The bullets were real, the deaths were real, the billowing black smoke and the flames were real. But it all looked like a scene from a Bruce Willis action movie. Suddenly the SAS was front-page news. It did not please the regiment which until then could easily have been tagged the Secret Air Service. This elite squad had been dragged reluctantly into the public eye. Since their formation during the Second World War this regiment, formed by the legendary Colonel David Stirling to penetrate enemy lines and use small teams of highly-trained men to strike against enemy airfields and supply lines, had conducted many successful operations unknown to the man in the street or indeed to many politicians and other soldiers.

The London embassy siege was a messy affair. Different factions involved in Iranian politics were at war with each other inside the building, resulting in revolutionaries taking hostages, killing one of them and threatening to spill even more blood. All this on the then Prime Minister Margaret Thatcher's doorstep, watched on TV news bulletins for several days by millions round the world. The Iron Lady needed to stop it. So she turned to the SAS. And in seventeen dramatic and violent minutes they ended it. Codenamed "Operation Nimrod," the attack by the SAS on the embassy was broadcast live on prime-time TV on a bank holiday Monday evening. It did wonders for Thatcher's reputation as a decisive politician unafraid to take violent action if there was no other alternative.

Incidentally, being at the scene did no harm either to the careers of several journalists, in particular Kate Aidie, who was a BBC duty reporter at the time of the attack and went on to become a top war-zone correspondent, often reporting direct to camera in the front line as bullets flew.

The TV coverage also led to a huge number of applications from soldiers wanting to join the SAS. One insider remarked that some of the would-be members "were convinced that a balaclava and a Heckler and Koch sub-machine gun would be handed to them over the counter" and they could go off right away and get down to the business of breaking up embassy-style sieges on a regular basis!

Terrorists inside the building were captured and killed by the soldiers. This led to a couple of SAS men being accused of unnecessarily killing two men in the embassy but they were later cleared and the killings deemed legal. All the resulting publicity and debate about whether or not the government's actions had been appropriate meant that however much they did not want it, the regiment had been forced into the public arena and earned a fearsome reputation for speedy action and military efficiency. Days of deadlock had ended in minutes and that ruthless speed of action was to become an SAS hallmark.

In one of those odd coincidences that can mark a life, a man who went on to become a controversial Chief Inspector of Prisons in Scotland – and a critic of conditions in Peterhead and other Scottish prisons – was involved in the London action as a soldier earlier in his career. Clive Fairweather was in the SAS at the time and he was second in command of the hostage rescue operation. From the regiment's head-quarters in Herefordshire he coordinated support for the operation and played a major role in its success. He was one of the top brass in the army unhappy about the action playing out on TV in real time. He was of the opinion that the army should have taken the media into its confidence by

136

revealing the plans in return for a temporary news blackout. He and others in the regiment wanted their operations to continue to be secret and not turn soldiers into celebrities of any kind.

An unusual man, Fairweather, the son of a policeman, was no respecter of rules, a trait that emerged early in his life when he was "asked" to leave George Heriot's school allegedly for the "sake of the staff and pupils." But his streak of "bolshiness" did no harm to his army career, which was highly successful. In 1987 he took over command of the 1st KOSB based in West Berlin, where he dealt with a bullying scandal involving sadistic initiation rites. In his final army days he was a colonel in the Scottish division based in Edinburgh Castle. A year later he accepted an invitation from Scottish Secretary Ian Lang to become Chief Inspector of Prisons. Perhaps the Tory politician had taken account of his success in Berlin.

Fairweather did not mess about in his new job and produced a damning series of reports on Scottish prisons. Politicians and prison governors did not like what they read. He was an early critic of slopping out and was not in favour of any privatisation. In particular, later in his career he opposed moves to close Peterhead with its then ground-breaking sex offenders unit. In the army and in the prison service this remarkable man made many headlines. His prison career ended in a paper storm of black type headlines in tabloids and broadsheets alike when it emerged that when his contract ran out in 2002 he was not to be reappointed. Too honest a man for the politicians, it would seem.

There can be little doubt that the success of the London action emboldened the Iron Lady to authorise another similar SAS hit seven years later in Peterhead Prison. No cameras or TV commentary this time and the mission to end a prison riot took only around six minutes. Unlike the action in London, there were no deaths or serious injury. This time the public were not allowed to watch from the comfort of their armchairs and the full story took years to emerge. Sometimes it was even denied the SAS were involved. It was a classic example of using minimum force and no firearms to save the life of a prison officer who had been taken hostage by violent cons, something that is a daily nightmare scenario for anyone in the prison service.

1987 had been a bad year in Scotland's prisons. There had been serious unrest in establishments all over the country. It was as if some sinister troublemaking virus was spreading from one jail to another. Peterhead, in the midst of a long-running violent war between inmates and staff, was an obvious location for an outbreak. It was not called The Hate Factory for nothing. Years of violence and counter-violence had destroyed morale and any relationship between detained and detainers. On occasion a cliché is an accurate way to describe something and the words "ticking" and "time bomb" and "pressure" and "pot" fit the bill here. Prisoners have plenty of time to follow in the press or on the radio or TV what is going on in other prisons and the hard men "up north" were well aware of riotous happenings in Barlinnie earlier in the year and figured that a similar spectacular protest would highlight what they felt were the bad conditions in their jail at that time.

Peterhead had been nicknamed The Hate Factory for years. Some even called it Scotland's gulag, a prison of no hope. The nicknames were a minor issue compared to what was to come. In a reality check for the prison service and the country in general, suddenly mayhem broke out. The real hatred from both sides became physical. There was not one trigger issue that started it. It was like a collective attack of what the police often call "going bersi." Berserk it was.

Without warning, the prisoners started tearing the place apart en masse. One of the leading figures in the violence was Sammy "The Bear" Ralston, an armed robber and a troublemaker over the years in many a Scottish prison. His part in the Peterhead affair cost him an extra seven years on an already lengthy sentence, but he had twice before been convicted of mobbing and rioting in prison. Recently he gave the *Scottish Sun* some insight on how he and others felt at the start of this particular riot: "I needed to get all my anger out so I smashed a few windows. That made me feel a bit better." The prisoners had made makeshift balaclavas out of bandages and rags, and on the rampage they were a fearsome crew.

Around fifty dangerous prisoners, murderers and rapists among them, facing long, long sentences had nothing to lose. They seized control of D Block and worked out their hatred of the place and their jailors in an orgy of destruction. Initially there was some hope that they could be calmed down after they had got the violence out of their systems. Remarkably most of the fifty did indeed surrender to their captors after the initial flow of the adrenalin that was pumping through their blood eased. This was not an option for a hard core of around five prisoners – Ralston, Douglas Mathewson, and Malcolm Leggat among them – lifers incarcerated for violent crimes, desperate men who had in the past taken all the discipline the prison service could throw at them. And maybe also suffered some violence against them that was not what you might call legal.

In the 1980s Peterhead had tough men in the cells and

139

tough men in uniform. The hard core of rioters resisted any call to join the mass surrender and they had a strong card to play – they had taken a prison officer hostage. They retreated to an area high in the roof space of the old prison and created all sorts of barricades and booby traps that prevented the authorities getting anywhere near them for five days. That is a long time in a riot. Using burning bedding, bedpans and anything else they could find, they kept the guards away from them. Their lair was like a medieval castle under siege with a wall of debris and wreckage acting as the moat. All sorts of debris, slates and anything else that could be got to hand were hurled down on the prison officers trying to break the riot.

Their unfortunate hostage was a veteran prison officer, at fifty-six no doubt looking forward to a pleasant retirement in rural Aberdeenshire. The guard, Jackie Stuart, was snatched as the cons fled to their rooftop eyrie. He had gone to the aid of a fellow officer who was under attack and was snatched by the ringleaders as they fled to the attic. It was an unfortunate choice by the rioters, for Jackie had only one kidney and needed daily medical attention and drugs to keep him healthy. This was an extra inducement for the authorities to get him to safety ASAP. It was a complication that helped make Mrs Thatcher in faraway London take the decisive step of calling in the SAS after days when the riot dominated the news in print and on TV, days that Ralston and Co kept the authorities at bay. The prison officers simply could not get to them. And the protestors had even cruelly dragged Jackie Stuart up out of their attic rat's nest to parade him on the rooftop to taunt and enrage his helpless colleagues down on the ground. It is a testament to the sort of character Jackie was that in retirement in 2012, long years after his ordeal, he could appear in a television interview and with a wry smile recall the horrors of that day. The BBC had footage of Jackie being hauled out of the attic on to the rooftop, where a hooded prisoner swung a weapon at his head. There was no doubt that the troublemakers meant business. It could have cost a life.

Scottish politicians and the men at the top of the Scottish prison service were goaded by public opinion to bring this outrage to an end and to ensure there were no deaths. But they faced a dilemma. The use of the army in a civilian matter was not at all usual. And, as is always the case, there were conflicting opinions. The hardliners wanted to turn to London for help immediately, as they feared for Jackie Stuart's life. Others were wary of the implication of ending the riot by bringing in the army. In the end they did turn to London and a prime minister who all Britain knew was not the sort of person to pussyfoot around. Mrs Thatcher, Malcolm Rifkind and Douglas Hurd gave the go-ahead for the SAS to intervene. A factor in Thatcher's decision was that this defiance of law and order was taking place on the eve of the Tory party conference. The Premier liked to wrap herself in the approval of public opinion and it did not look good that lawlessness was at large in one of Her Majesty's prisons. As in the London embassy siege, she wanted a solution and wanted it quickly.

The SAS were her "get out of jail" card and the end of the siege was dramatic. One eyewitness recently told me his memories of this secret and sudden action almost a quarter of a century ago. This experienced officer was working in another prison at the time, but he had vital knowledge of the fabric and layout of Peterhead and had served there. He could be very valuable to the SAS in their attempt to free the hostage and end the riot. He knew every nook and cranny in the prison. He was attending a 9am meeting of heads of departments in his then current prison billet. By chance another old Peterhead executive was also there. They had no inkling how their lives were to change that day when the phone rang with the latest news of the desperate state of affairs up north and a dramatic request for them to get involved. These two guys were needed urgently. No one explained exactly why. They were just told to get ready immediately for a move north. Literally within minutes they were in an unmarked car heading for the scene of the action. The mystery trip and the speed of it all was unsettling. This prison service veteran, now enjoying a quiet retirement, told me it was the journey of a lifetime. There was no chitchat between the driver, his colleague and the two passengers, who by now had guessed they would soon be involved in perhaps the most dramatic siege in Scottish prison history. Pleasantries on the weather, the passing scenery and such like were clearly out!

It was a high-speed drive through towns and villages. At every traffic light, or possible slow spot, there was a police presence. The car sped northwards unimpeded by speed limits or traffic lights. For the occupants it was a real life thrill ride that had the adrenalin pumping and the imagination working overtime.

At the prison itself, events were moving fast. The prisoners were still in the loft blockading the stairs with any debris they could find. The prison officers could not get near enough to the rioters to control the situation. But the stand-off was nearing a dramatic conclusion. As the two prison service veterans were being ushered into a conference with the senior executives of the prison, a group of 4x4s were leaving a nearby old airfield. The passengers had descended from a Hercules military transport aircraft which had flown them from Hereford and they were whisked to the back door of the prison. Suddenly about twenty tough-looking guys in fatigues and carrying what looked like cricket bags full of kit were in the prison. The Peterhead staff mostly did not know who they were. But they had the authorisation to enter the jail and immediately talked to the men running the operation against the holed-up prisoners. The atmosphere was chilling. The hit squad wore trainers rather than boots to facilitate walking across the slippery roof tiles, they had flash-bang gas canisters and gas masks. They were armed and dangerous. The "cricket" bags did not contain linseed-oiled bats but staves of the sort that would have come in handy in a Glasgow gang fight.

There was no attempt at good mornings or any small talk or handshaking as they burst into the makeshift HQ of the prison officers attempting to control the riot, now in its fifth day. My eyewitness told me wryly that manners were not in the skill set of these guys. They clearly had a job to do. The newcomers called each other by their first names or nicknames, there was no sergeant this or captain that. It was Andy, Bill and Matt or whatever. They fizzed with energy and exuded competence. Ladders and ropes were also in the kit. And explosives.

The prison officer who knew most about the layout of the prison was grabbed and pushed in front of a long deep window that spanned two or three storeys, ending up just below the attic and quizzed, "What is that frame made of?"

"Cast iron, I think," he replied but that did not wash with the newcomers.

"Don't think – tell us what it is made of," they snapped aggressively.

He stuck with cast iron and in seconds ladders were up

143

the wall and "gelly" placed round the frame and it was swiftly blown out, leaving access to the upper floors. The need for speed was heightened by the fact that some prisoners in other parts of the jail had spotted something going on and were shouting warnings to the men in the attic. Even after the window had been blown out the access to where the hostage was held involved walking along slippery ridge tiles.

A forward squad of four of the SAS men launched themselves into action, dragging their sticks and weapons up into the roof of the prison and letting off stun grenades. They attacked the rioters, wielding the staves with expert violence and taping the prisoners up as they fell. When the rioters were safely restrained the men in fatigues simply left them there on the floor to be sorted out by the prison service. They spent little time talking to the Scottish police and headed back to their waiting aircraft. The whole action had lasted less than a quarter of an hour, the climax taking just a few minutes. The rescuers who had very possibly saved the life of the hostage were back at their HQ in England in time for a second breakfast. There was no triumphalism before they left Peterhead as speedily as they had arrived. Dangerous men themselves, they had brought a daring end to the siege. My eyewitness said he had never seen anything so scary or so effective in his life. But the atmosphere changed when the time came for him to return south – and he was given a train ticket for his trouble. No high-speed secret service limo this time. But he had witnessed history.

Recently the second-in-command of the SAS operation told the *Daily Record*'s Maggie Barry what it was like viewed from the army side. He said it was quite a technical operation, in which "we had to do explosive entries into different wings of the prison" and seven or eight guys had to walk along the parapet of the roof on a ledge only a few feet wide. All this in the pitch dark. His story of the breaking up of the riot was low-key, as you might expect from a soldier. Indeed one of his memories of that dramatic day was that he would not forget it, as on the Saturday he was due to play squash for the army in Portsmouth and had to cancel it, thus ruining his weekend!

But even years after the SAS men had returned south in their "Hercs" this remarkable episode was not completely over. It would be the subject of rumour and speculation for years before the real story eventually emerged. And, as in the London siege before it, the secretive SAS were dragged into a court case and further details of the rescue of the hostages came into the public arena. In January 1993, six years after the event, a claim for £30,000 damages by thirty-two-year-old John Devine was heard in the Court of Session in Edinburgh. One of the SAS squad flown so dramatically to the prison to end the siege was accused of "setting out to teach the prisoners a lesson." The soldier was only identified as "T" and he said, "It was not true that his attitude was whatever you do with prison warders you do not monkey around with the SAS." Devine had made the cash claim against the by then Secretary of State for Scotland Ian Lang. The court was told that one prison officer had been a hostage for more than 100 hours (Jackie Stuart) and another had also been held as a hostage and sustained a broken ankle and was released.

Court 8 was a bizarre scene. It was divided by a seven-foot-high screen to hide the identity of Soldier T. The soldier said he was trained to deal with counter-terrorism incidents and that he was an expert in the release of hostages. He said

145

that on arrival at the prison he and his fellow SAS men were briefed that the rioters holed up in D Hall were dangerous and they were shown photographs of them to help identify them. He said his squad were given batons, gas canisters and flash-bang grenades. It was decided that "T" and six others would break through a hatch in the roof of the hall. This was about 3am and it was still dark. They were near to the hatch when prisoners in other parts of the jail saw them and started shouting warnings to the ringleaders. Soldier T told Alastair Dunlop, QC for the Secretary of State, that this "compromised" the mission. At this point the soldiers got the go-ahead to attack and dropped two flash-bang grenades into the hatch and "T" entered first with a torch to use in the dark.

He told the court: "As I entered the attic space I came across the prison warder. I moved towards him and checked that he was okay and he was just passed behind me to the next person." He then said that almost instantly he saw a rioter coming towards him, apparently with a knife in his hand. "I moved towards him and struck his forearm and then struck upwards to strike his face. The first blow was to disarm and the second was to enable me to move closer and put him off his balance." He denied striking the prisoner about the head with a baton at any other stage and said that the prisoner was not thrown twelve feet from the attic to the gallery below. Cross-examined by the legendary QC Lionel Daiches, he denied saying or hearing his colleagues say, "You're going for a spin, pal."

The lawyer than said, "Weren't you absolutely certain you were going to teach him a lesson, the sort he would remember?"

Soldier T relied firmly, "No."

When Mr Daiches suggested that Mr Devine's head was being "burst open" when he was not opposing the SAS in any way, the answer was again a firm no.

When the court resumed the next day John Devine's claim was thrown out. The jury took a mere thirty minutes to reject his civil action for his alleged injuries in the affair. But the defeated party took some satisfaction, if not money, from the court action. Devine's lawyer, Cameron Fyfe, said, "The fact that the case proceeded to court, and in particular to a jury, is for him a victory in itself. For years the authorities refused to admit that the SAS was used to bring the Peterhead siege to an end." He went on to say his client wanted him to highlight his frustration in getting the case to court. "We came up against a great deal of resistance and Mr Devine was granted legal aid only at the last minute. This situation should not be allowed to arise again."

Later it was confirmed that Jimmy Boyle, the controversial convicted killer who went on to a career as a sculptor and artist via the Barlinnie Special Unit and who had caused so much trouble in Peterhead himself, had helped financially in the legal costs in bringing the case to court. Boyle said after the conclusion of the case that the main principle of the case was established "that the SAS were held accountable for their actions in open court." That was a highly personal verdict and one that might not have the support of those who have had their lives saved in the actions, many unpublicised, by the Special Air Service.

147

11

FIRE AND HELL IN A-HALL

One of the pleasures of historical research is uncovering the nuggets of massive understatement contained in the official records. The newspapers' habit of calling the prison The Hate Factory says a lot about Peterhead in a few words. No understatement there. Years of violence between prisoners and their jailors, riots, dirty protests, it is all encompassed in the nickname. The prison service now, rightly, on the eve of the opening of a new super jail on a site adjacent to the old one, does not hide from the facts but it does put it a bit more delicately. Officially it says, "Peterhead has had a somewhat troubled history, not least the number of disturbances and rooftop protests in the late 1980s." Too true, and the story of the SAS intervention may have been unique but it happened during one riot of many. And the ordeal of Jackie Stuart was not a solitary happening.

The previous year in November 1986 there had been another dangerous riot in the prison and again a warder was taken hostage. This time he was John Crossan and he was, like Jackie, extremely lucky to escape with his life and survive the incident physically uninjured, though he was held by desperate knife-wielding men for four days of mental torture. I am always concerned that so often the survivors of hostage taking are described in newspaper reports as "unhurt" – as if the mental anguish of being held blindfolded with a knife at your throat was not an injury. At times Mr Crossan's captors threatened that they would cut his fingers off. And perhaps worse.

It began on a Sunday and ended on a Thursday. Previous to the actual riot there had been a disturbing feeling in the prison that all was far from normal. The officers in A Hall had, it seems, been warned that it was best to patrol in twos if possible. The closed environment of a prison can magnify rumours and emotions and brew up fears. The men who ran the prison were convinced that trouble lay ahead. John Crossan was the unlucky one taken hostage by convicted murderers who had knives as weapons.

What lit the torch paper? As in the case of the later SAS riot, who really knows? As in most prison riots the pressure pot blows open in something of a spontaneous outbreak of violence. Bad blood between jailer and jailed simply erupts. At the trial of the hostage takers in Peterhead High Court, Mr Crossan denied that prison officers in riot gear had been beating their sticks noisily against their shields outside A Hall as claimed by inmates. It was remarked at the trial that it would be most unusual for officers to be in riot gear before the riot even started! John Crossan also denied that when the trouble did start the officers sprinted for the exits and he had simply been left behind. Three lifers, Andrew Walker, William Ballantyne and John Smith, were convicted for their part in the riot and ten years to be served concurrently were added to their sentences, and these new convictions were to be taken into account when the possibility of parole came up. The three admitted mobbing and rioting and seizing John Crossan and blindfolding him. The three accused also admitted assaulting fifteen officers by forcing them to leave A Hall by threatening their colleague. And to setting fire to A Hall and causing damage that cost more than a quarter of a million pounds to put right.

A fourth convict called Anderson was found not guilty, which resulted in John Smith laughing and declaring, "That is a burden off my shoulders." Earlier in the trial he had shouted out in court that this particular jail mate was innocent. Smith was an interesting man and in his defence Donald Robertson QC read out a letter his client had written. In it there is much insight into the thinking of prisoners and the appalling conditions in Peterhead at the time. Lord Murray the judge was told: "Can anyone ever understand the horrors of prison without being part of it, feeling the anxieties of it, knowing the helplessness, living in desolation? Prison life does not provide the creative environment and training needed for a man to make a new beginning on the outside. Instead it is geared to using the men as labour, punishing if necessary and disregard [sic] their inner spirit as of no consequence. Physical and mental brutality does exist in Peterhead. This matter can only be resolved with the introduction of rehabilitation. If the prison authorities insist on treating prisoners like animals then prisoners will continue to act like animals. Prisoners, including myself, have been described as incurable psychopaths, subversive and hell-bent on destruction. This can only be described as an excuse rather than a truth. I ask you, have prisoners been given the chance to express themselves in any other way? Certainly not in Peterhead."

Some of this is clearly predictable pleading, but some of

it contains confirmation that around twenty-five years ago Peterhead was not in the van of any movement to turn lives around rather than simply punish the guilty. Indeed the happenings inside Peterhead had long been a driving force for those who wanted a new approach to dealing with long-term prisoners. For years, even back in the 1970s, trouble in Peterhead had helped to lead to the founding of the Barlinnie Special Unit, where the emphasis was on releasing any internal creativity to be found in a hardened criminal. Sadly, as we know, that admirable experiment in prison reform foundered precisely because it went too far too fast in the opposite direction to the public's perception of what prison life should be. But "up north" The Hate Factory was churning out haters and those labelled animals did indeed behave like animals.

All that was many years ago but it is dispiriting to find that today not all that much has changed. Of course there are now peaceful ways for prisoners to air grievances, and training for release has increased and conditions inside are more carefully monitored. Prison officers too are now well trained in rehabilitation. But there are still massive differences in the way some British prisons operate compared to what goes on elsewhere.

In the spring of 2013 Erwin James, an ex-con turned perceptive commentator on prison affairs for *The Guardian*, visited an Oslo fjord to report on life on the Norwegian prison island of Bastoy. This is a place to give Britain's massive army of hangers and floggers, the lock 'em up and throw away the key brigade, apoplexy. The prisoners include murderers and drug smugglers who live with a degree of freedom on the island, growing their own food, running a stable and a bicycle repair shop (many of the cons

151

have their own bikes). There are no drugs, no booze, and no women – except for a few uniformed prison officers – and no children. And no escape from the island, though the cons even run the ferry to and from the mainland. It is a life of training for re-entry into the community. Compared with life even today in British prisons it is hard to avoid the word "cushy." However, Erwin James spoke to the governor who told him – surprise, surprise – that if you treated people like animals they behaved like animals. They don't do that on Bastoy. But the most remarkable fact about Bastoy is that it has the lowest reoffending rate of any prison in Europe. Something to think about?

That Scottish prison riot back in 1986 at least had the effect of turning the spotlight on the prisoners' grievances, something eloquently highlighted by Ballantyne's QC, the redoubtable Ian Hamilton. He said the riot had started from a long series of grievances, real or imagined, and in his opinion there were insufficient channels for these grievances to be aired: "It seems to be the case at Peterhead prison the method for the ventilation of grievances was, and perhaps still is, insufficient and as a result of this they festered on until they resulted in the action and crimes on which your lordship has to pass sentence." He said he believed there existed adequate means of protecting officers and that since the riot his client has been confined in a cage in Porterfield Prison, Inverness, for twenty-four hours a day. He said Ballantyne expected that after being sentenced he would spend at least another six months but probably two years in one of the cages.

Ian Hamilton went on to describe the cage in the following terms: "The cage consists of a concrete box seven paces by five paces. The front of the box has iron bars, hence the name. On the 'public' side is a passage about a pace wide. The inmate is left there twenty-four hours a day. Since November [*it was now March*] the prisoner has not left the cage for exercise or ablutions. Excretion is into a chamber pot left in the cage and only slopped out once a day. The light is on twenty-four hours a day." Ian Hamilton went on to say that no one could face with equanimity what his client expected was going to happen to him for at least six months. He added: "However low these people may be and however necessary it may be to ostracise them from the intercourse and company of us, they are not animals. They should not have cried for help the way they did. But one question is left – what other way did they have to cry for help?"

Dr Kathy Charles of Edinburgh Napier University, a highly respected psychologist in the field of forensic psychology, told me: "The cage and regime described by Ian Hamilton is an environment that many people would feel unsuitable for animals, never mind human prisoners. Hearing such a description from a comfortable and unbiased position will almost always provoke shock and disdain. However, when John Smith asked if 'anyone could ever understand the horrors of prison without being part of it,' two kinds of insight can emerge. I'm sure he intended people to ponder what it is like to be a prisoner feeling powerless and desperate, but one could also consider what it might feel like in prison for staff who have to face the most dangerous and challenging people in society – every day and all in one place. Dreadful though the cage is, it is possible to imagine how such a hateful environment could have caused prison staff to come to believe that this extreme form of detention and deprivation was suitable. At their wits end and confronted with unpredictable barbarity and

153

violence, complete restriction of freedom and expression must have seemed a very attractive solution.

"Psychology is full of examples of how groups of individuals can lose perspective and make extreme choices when their reference to the wider environment is closed off. This is the case for both prisoners and prison staff. The prison, especially Peterhead and especially in years gone by, is so different to everyday life that normal standards of behaviour, reasoning and decision-making change. Coupled with the very obvious power disparity between a prisoner and a jailor, this unnatural environment is bound to result in extreme deviation from what would be considered as normal by most people. Treating people like animals in a cage seems barbaric by our calm and reasoned standards but would it still feel so distasteful if we'd been in the same pressure cooker that led to its creation?

"I imagine very few, if any, psychologists would be able to justify the kind of environment described and experienced in 1980s Peterhead prison. I can certainly offer no argument for it. It is impossible to see how any person could emerge from such an environment as a reformed character better equipped to live a productive and law abiding life. Nevertheless, it is quite uncomfortable for many people to accept that 'nicer' prisons actually result in lower rates of reoffending. When asked if prisons should rehabilitate offenders most people answer yes, yet if they hear about what that entails (often being 'nice' and giving people chances to demonstrate change and creativity), they often don't like it at all. Simultaneously punishing and rehabilitating someone is a difficult task. The loss of liberty is supposed to be the punishment, what happens inside the prison is supposed to rehabilitate not further punish and humiliate.

"Certain types of offender are undoubtedly regarded as animals by the media and many members of the public. This belief can seem like a good justification for treating them like animals. In many cases the offender has already been treated like an animal in his home or community. It is true that not every offender has had a terrible life, some offenders commit crime simply because they find it exciting and a good source of income, but the high percentage of the prison population who have been physically, emotionally and sexually abused as children and adolescents can't be ignored. Somebody has to break the cycle of treating a person like an animal and then punishing their animal-like responses. If you pack men into cages with no form of expression, no facility to change, and no feeling of safety they will indeed behave like animals."

There are no easy answers to an issue that our society has been arguing over both before and since Peterhead prison was built in the nineteenth century. However, most civilised people will be thankful that the cages, like iron shackles, are now consigned to history along with other barbaric practices of the past.

12

CHAMBER POTS AND BOMBS THROWN OUT OF CELL WINDOWS

As the very early history of the construction of Peterhead shows, some thought was given to saving building costs by the use of dry toilets rather than installing half-decent plumbing. I use the phrase "half-decent" with care since from day one toilet facilities in the jail have been less than adequate and you wonder what it would have been like if the bean counters of the 1880s had their way. However, even the primitive sanitation provided was only available during the times prisoners were not locked in the cells. At night there were no in-cell toilets or indeed washing facilities. The convicts sat on buckets or chamber pots and the malodorous mixture lay untouched till the morning and the unpleasant business of "slopping out." This was a procedure involving the warders supervising the emptying of the containers into sluicing drains. No wonder it has been often remarked that you could tell a prison warder from the marks of a clothes peg on the nose.

When the planners were considering the provision of toilets in Peterhead they should have looked across the

Irish Sea for inspiration. When it opened in 1850, almost forty years before Peterhead was built, Mountjoy Prison in Dublin had a flushing toilet in each cell. This, however, is remarkable considering that the Irish penal system had some establishments still slopping out as late as 2009. In England and Wales slopping out was abolished in 1996 in all but a few establishments. In Scotland the process of removing this degrading process began as far back as 1994 when the European Committee for the Prevention of Torture condemned slopping out in Barlinnie – and it also criticised overcrowding and the long hours some prisoners were incarcerated in their cells. The committee published many opinions about the "unacceptable" conditions in Scottish prisons. Not surprisingly, they also criticised the use of the tiny dogbox cells described earlier, now confined to history, where prisoners were held as they were processed for admission to the prison.

In prisons time passes slowly and the authorities in general and the law in particular also move at a snail's pace. So not much happened between 1994 and 2001. The real catalyst for change was a petition in that year by a prisoner called Robert Napier, who claimed in essence that slopping out breached his human rights. It is interesting that even today "human rights" for prisoners is still highly controversial. Particularly with the current controversy on whether or not they should be allowed the vote. Napier's case was heard by Lord Bonomy and it was an eye-opener for those in the public unaware just how primitive prison sanitation could be.

In support of Napier, international experts in prisons were brought before the Court of Session in Edinburgh. Medical experts, nutritionists, psychologists and psychiatrists gave the court the benefit of their views. Lord Bonomy found that the "triple vices" of a poor regime, overcrowding and slopping out did breach the prisoner's rights. Napier was awarded damages. This was the case that really started the ball rolling and for years after it there was claim and counter-claim and many lawyers made a good living representing hundreds of avaricious prisoners trying to claw their way onto a fast-moving cash bandwagon.

Lord Bonomy's judgement spelled out just how barbaric slopping out was and its effect on prisoners. It seemed less concerned about the effect on the prison officers who, with some logic, could have pointed out that the practice could also be said to have infringed their human rights. The Court of Session case was concerned with what was going on in Barlinnie but the deeply unpleasant facts it exposed applied equally to other jails such as Peterhead. Perhaps more so in Peterhead, where toilet facilities were way behind the norm acceptable in the prison service. Bonomy wrote that "the core element of slopping out – emptying the containers – was a chaotic event, particularly in the morning." He mentioned that at the end of each flat in the prison halls there were three showers, four lavatories, six urinals and fourteen wash hand basins, for the use of up to eighty prisoners on the flat. There were also two ceramic sluices in which pris-oners could dispose of the contents of their chamber pots and urine bottles; they could also use the lavatories for that purpose. Each sluice had hot and cold running water taps and a flush mechanism. Next to each of the sluices was a ceramic Belfast sink, the waste from which also ran into the sluice. The pots and bottles could be rinsed in either. In June 2001 a tank had been installed to provide disinfectant solu-tion for the sluice, but was not in use. Disinfectant tablets were issued to prisoners when they were first admitted to C Hall. Though there was some dispute on how readily available they were.

Bonomy painted a detailed and horrific picture of the process: the Hall began to come to life at about 6.30am. "The first task for officers was to establish that all prisoners were still present and relay that information to a central control. It was only once every prisoner in the prison had been accounted for that cells began to be unlocked. Those who had to attend court were released first. Thereafter the cells generally were unlocked, about a quarter at a time. The order in which they were unlocked was rotated so that every four days each prisoner would be in the first batch. There was some overlap, but generally speaking the next quarter were released after most of the previous quarter had been locked up again. Prisoners had about fifteen to twenty minutes, and sometimes less, to slop out and use the facilities at the arches.

"The whole process was intended to be completed at about 8am. As a result, between fifteen and twenty prisoners would descend upon the ablutions area together, all carrying a number of items: their urine bottles and chamber pots, where appropriate, to be emptied; cutlery and plates to be rinsed, either at the Belfast sink or the sluice; a water bottle to be filled with drinking water from a tap adjacent to the wash hand basins; possibly a rubbish basket to be emptied; and a towel and personal toiletry items. This was the only occasion on which a prisoner was permitted to take a towel to the ablutions. Each prisoner had a basin and a jug which he could also take to the arches and fill with water to use in his cell for washing later. The last prisoners from the previous group might also still be there. Each had then

159

to slop out, wash/shower, shave and go to the lavatory as necessary."

The evidence in general confirmed the petitioner's description of the process as a "free-for-all." Queues built up to use the various facilities, particularly the sluices and the showers, since there were only two and three respectively. An officer was on duty to take bookings for telephone calls, issue razor blades, take letters, note requests to attend the nurse, social worker or dentist, and note requests to attend PT, for which there was a very limited number of places. Bonomy said, "I was left with the clear impression that everything was done in a rush and under pressure."

And he went on: "Although the petitioner [Napier] never had to empty a chamber pot, it was plain, from his evidence and the evidence of other prisoners and prison staff, that on a daily basis a significant number of chamber pots were emptied as each group of prisoners went to the arches. Each of the other prisoners who gave evidence used his chamber pot and also had a cell mate who did. Most prisoners also had urine bottles to empty. There was a practice among prisoners of putting faeces into plastic bags with a view to minimising the smell in the cell. In the past these had been thrown from cell windows to improve the atmosphere within the cells. By May 2001 a mesh covering had been placed outside each cell window to prevent this practice. [*In Peterhead where the bags were also hurled out of the windows the practice was known as "bombing."*] With the option of throwing the bags out the window removed, prisoners would instead attempt to flush these bags down the lavatories. As a result, lavatories would become blocked and overflow.

"Not every prisoner would flush the sluice after depositing material there, resulting in an accumulation which was slow to clear and could cause a blockage and overflow. Although the petitioner did not mention such overflows occurring, there was other evidence from prisoners and staff which led me to conclude that blockages and the resultant overflow were a problem throughout the Hall. A strong, foul smell of a mixture of urine and excrement permeated the arches. The hot water taps were often left running into the sluices and the heat and steam appeared to exacerbate the smell. The petitioner described the arches as 'stinking' and the smell as 'strong, not gut-wrenching but not far off.' As a result of the number of prisoners carrying several items converging on and leaving the ablutions area simultaneously, there were often collisions and spillages which might contaminate the shoes, clothing or skin of a passing prisoner."

Prisoners who gave evidence described the atmosphere at slopping out as "stinking" and the smell as "awful" and "incredible." Bonomy said, "These descriptions were not challenged. Indeed they were confirmed by the evidence of staff."

These were the sort of appalling conditions endured by prisoners and staff in Scotland's jails before, finally, slopping out became just a bitter memory. The installation of proper toilets and washing facilities in cells took many years and in 2004 prisoners in five of Scotland's sixteen jails were still slopping out. Budget cuts and the physical difficulties in putting plumbing into small cells contributed to the delays. When slopping out ended in HM Young Offenders Institution in Polmont in 2007, it left Peterhead as the only jail where prisoners did not have access to decent sanitation. The old granite fortress beside the North Sea was in an unenviable position of having hundreds of men using chemical toilets after lock-up.

Largely to blame for pushing PHead to the bottom of the sanitary league was the fact that it had been constructed out of the world-famous local granite and that made it well-nigh impossible to drill through walls and partitions to install decent plumbing. Not so, of course, in the new prison rising up next door, where the design grows from a blank page. This will make it a huge improvement for the current staff who work in poor, cramped conditions. Many told me they can hardly wait till the new place opens. Having witnessed the cramped reception and educational area I am not surprised. But when HMP Grampian does finally open there will undoubtedly be an outcry in the media and sarcastic remarks about HMP Hilton when the public are introduced to the new place by feature writers and TV cameramen.

Indeed, a taste of what was to come arrived many months before the opening of the new prison, when it was disclosed that it would have under-floor heating. The prison service spokeswoman making the announcement said, "The selection of an under-floor heating system to provide all the cells in the accommodation blocks with heat was proposed to allow the best use of renewable heat energy." Sounds sensible but only hours after the statement was issued headlines like "Toastie Toes" were rolling off the presses. Maybe some of the accusations will be justified, but surely no one can mourn the passing of scenes like those above so eloquently described by Lord Bonomy in his judgement in the game-changing case brought to the Court of Session by prisoner Robert Napier.

13

SICKENING STENCH, BODY ARMOUR AND DIRTY PROTESTS

Slopping out was far from the only – to coin a phrase – torture by toilet in Peterhead. Since the early 1980s the so-called dirty protests filled the pages of newspapers with accounts of prisoners smearing themselves and the walls of their cells with excrement and urinating everywhere and anywhere. At its height you could almost smell the stench and feel the creeping dampness in the newspaper in your hands. When much of what happened in its 125-year history is long forgotten the memory of the dirty protests will still attract comment.

Newspapers are a natural target for accusations of exaggeration. And often the charge can be sustained. Not, however, in the case of dirty protest, a phrase that somehow vaguely sanitises what it was actually like. However vivid the second-hand stories of the dirty protests in the late 1960s, '70s and '80s were, they could not fully convey the horror of what was going on in the cells that held the dangerous Category A prisoners, around twenty of them at one time.

Now empty and waiting for demolition, these cells held

the most dangerous and desperate men in the jail. Looking at them today in disrepair and abandoned to history it is hard not to resort to the old cliché "if stones could speak." The men caged here were the haters supreme in The Hate Factory. Some had an admitted ambition – to kill a prison officer. Or maybe two. An unguarded moment could produce an attack or hostage taking from the men held for years behind these bars without hope of release. As an officer you could not take your eyes off them for a minute. There was no time to relax when on duty in and around the cells of these particular cons. They were not there to do the time and keep their heads down or form cosy, chatty relationships with their jailers. They were out to fight, determined to kill if possible and, if not, to inflict the most violence they could.

The sentences being served by most of these guys were so long that an extra year or two for attacking an officer was of little consequence. Revenge and hatred were their motivation. Vile crimes when they were free to roam the streets of the worst areas in Scotland's great cities had put them away for years. They really had nothing to lose. The routine used by the warders in this area of the prison shows the depth of the hatred involved. Several times a day the cells had to be opened to allow the inmates to slop out. On each occasion the door was only opened when there were three officers in full riot gear there to make sure that if the caged and "animalised," as they would have it, occupant leapt at his captors in a crazed outburst of violence he would be subdued by force. On some occasions the warders, apart from face helmets and the other paraphernalia of riot gear, also had shields and staves. And they could be armed.

This was serious stuff. Many a prison officer in any jail in the country will tell you of regular "roll overs" in prisons

– occasions when an inmate takes a casual swing at a screw who he has a grudge with or some kind of issue and it all ends in a wrestling match. But roll overs did not last long and they were a million miles away from the hatred of those considered dangerous enough to be held under Rule 36, which allows the separation and different regime for prisoners deemed to be difficult. It should also be remembered that prisoners have a knack at making potentially dangerous weapons out of almost anything that comes to hand. Open the door of a cell in the toughest part of The Hate Factory and you could face a wild man with a makeshift knife, or someone intent on urinating all over you, spitting at you and attempting to prod you in the eye with a broomstick. Or make you handle his body, which he had covered in excrement, in order to restrain him.

Much has been made of so-called "batter squads" in Peterhead and there is no doubt in my mind that some did exist. But the provocation was enormous. That said, I was told by one long-serving and competent officer recently that in his career he never saw a prisoner battered.

One provocation that is seldom mentioned in all the tales of violence on both sides in the war in The Hate Factory and that only eased in its final years was the constant feeling of fear felt by the staff. Officers feared attack at every minute of their working lives. And there was the worse fear of being taken hostage. As we have seen, this was a not infrequent happening in HMP Peterhead down the years.

I listened to one officer with many years of service under his belt and he told me of his early days as the youngest officer in the prison. He knew the history of hostage taking and attacks against warders and it seemed to him that many of them were on young officers. The reason was simple: the most inexperienced were the most vulnerable. He spent some months worrying as the youngest officer in the place that he was top of the prison hit list. Then another new boy arrived and he felt almost guilty at the feeling of relief that he himself had moved a little way down the target list. It is remarkable that the simple act of unlocking a cell to let an inmate out for any purpose at all was so regimented and so dangerous. That this was so, however, is testified by the fact that practice simulations of dealing with this situation were a regular part of the officer training regime. But a simulation is a simulation and real urine and excrement is another matter. The dirty protesters did not simply take action when someone came knocking on the cell door. Left alone, they urinated and defected on the floor and the walls, smearing their own naked bodies.

One veteran officer told me that, quite naturally, you have a higher tolerance to the stench of your own waste. Someone else's is another matter altogether. And even if the culprit is removed from a dirty protest cell the trauma for officers is not over. Someone has to don a protective suit and hose the place down – not work much reported in the press, which at times seemed obsessed by any incidents of warders allegedly attacking cons. Provocation by piss and shit. It happened. And the reality of it underlined the sad fact that crime-fighting, or containing criminals, is not the glamorous occupation portrayed in countless lightweight TV series.

Jimmy Boyle is one of the most infamous of all Peterhead prisoners who is associated with the era of dirty protests. He has taken a lot of stick in the press and in books – some of it from me – on a perceived reluctance to apologise for his actions earlier in his life. The actions that put him into

The Hate Factory, and what he did there. He does not deny crime has many victims but the suggestion is teased into his story that he, too, is somehow a victim. It is all discussed in depth in his remarkable book, *A Sense of Freedom*. There is irony in the title Boyle chose – there was no freedom and there never will be for his victim. There is irony, too, in his comfortable existence as a much-vaunted sculptor.

In addition to his Peterhead experiences he spent many months naked in a tiny cell four feet by four feet by seven in Inverness before these inhuman "cages" were finally banned by authorities, sadly seemingly reluctantly and at the last possible moment, bowing rightfully to public opinion and common humanity. Now he can conduct interviews on a balcony under an African sun in Morocco with the Atlas Mountains in the skyline. It is a long way from the Gorbals, Porterfield and Peterhead and a long way from the life of his contemporaries in crime. Or indeed those who suffered from his days as a criminal. While, as we will see in more detail later, he suffered terribly in Peterhead and Inverness and many wrong things were done to him and others in the jails years ago, there are disturbing moments in his book as the one-time hard man of the Gorbals recounts his youthful life of crime. His home life and the trouble he gave his mother is described in almost touching detail and with real tenderness, contrasting sharply with his actions on the street. There is no tenderness or compassion in throwaway lines about taking an eye out of a rival in a gang fight. Or "cutting" rival gangsters. In particular a description of the first time he slashed anyone is deeply unsettling.

Apart from his book, Boyle also collaborated with play-wright Tom McGrath on a play called *The Hard Man*. It was a fictionalised account of his early life. He had been convicted of murder in 1967 – a charge he still denies – and his story told on stage had considerable critical success. A revival was directed by Phillip Breen, who travelled to Africa to interview Boyle on his new home turf. He gave *The Scotsman* a fascinating account of their meeting. Boyle talked of warders and their charges locked in a cycle of violence and retribution. The discussion touched on the belief that if you treat prisoners like animals, as noted before, they tend to act like animals. In this scenario his own violence is seen as a survival strategy.

In their chat Boyle has much good to say about the Barlinnie Special Unit and its ethos, which meant there was intellectual engagement with even the most vile murderers and violent criminals and a search to find any redeeming talent as well as simply stopping them reoffending. Clearly he is a different man now from the one who entered Peterhead and from day one felt what he describes as the hatred on both sides. That hatred is still there to some extent.

Some years after his release a senior officer thought it might be an idea for him to return and discuss with his captors his life in the jail. It was a controversial and brave move on the part of the prison officer who organised it. The meeting was hardly a sell-out. Many officers, senior and junior, chose not to attend. Bitter memories of the bad old days were too strong. I was told Boyle was listened to in virtual silence and there was no flood of questions when he ended. Did he apologise, I asked the man who organised the event. "Well, yes," was the answer . . . "though not in as many words." That is the complexity of Boyle. But at least he turned up. And at least he was asked to return to the prison.

His book is essential reading for anyone with an interest

in crime, its causes and prevention. And it gives an interesting view of the prison and life in it from a man who, no matter your opinion of him as a human being, is a good communicator. As a kid he was in and out of all sorts of supposedly reforming institutions for the would-be hard man. But reform was not on his agenda though it has to be acknowledged he was badly mistreated in some of these institutions in the tough old days before social work became a decently caring profession. Boyle was born into a criminal family, not uncommon in Glasgow. Indeed one Glasgow governor told me of guys who ended there doing time in cells occupied in the past by their fathers and grandfathers and maybe in one of the other halls in the Big Hoose in the east end where an uncle or two stayed awhile. Indeed Boyle was sent north to Peterhead largely to put distance between him and a brother who was facing a murder charge in Glasgow. Apart from his own murder charge, Boyle had been involved in shebeens and money lending and all sorts of gangsterism.

On arrival "up north" in 1967 he was straight into the punishment block described earlier. He was a Rule 36 con from day one, though he claimed he did not know the reason why. In these cells, smaller than normal, he claimed you could barely spread your hands wide. In the book he moans about the hostile attitude of warders, the constant tension between prisoners and staff. A regime that discouraged any unnecessary conversation.

He did, of course, find himself in the company of old friends from the Gorbals. But that was not a wholly welcome state of affairs, as at that time staff seemed to him to be prejudiced against prisoners from Scotland's toughest city. Not too surprising, since the Glaswegians could be described as the cream of the troublemakers, and they had a tendency to form into rival "teams" just like they did out on the streets. These mini gangs were constantly looking for fights. This sort of behind bars gangland was, of course, a major problem for the officers to deal with.

Boyle's first memories of Peterhead were of the noise of chamber pots bashing on doors. The warders' first memories of him would be defecating on the floor, urinating everywhere and anywhere and throwing away meals. He was, in his own words, a walking time bomb. And that bomb would go off with some regularity.

Boyle's hatred of his captors could be fearsome, and he was ready at every opportunity to use his fists. Thumping a prison warder brought out a heavy mob in coloured overalls and a beating, he says. It was a bit of a pattern in his life behind bars and he says he received many a beating in Inverness and Peterhead. But punishment for his violence seemed to have little effect. Punishment by the ordinary prison regime did nothing to alter his ways. He was beyond that. His stay behind bars was a catalogue of fighting the enemy – society in general and prison officers in particular.

The founding of the Barlinnie Special Unit which was the salvation of him and others was sparked by the astonishingly high level of attacks on officers and dirty protests in Peterhead. The press reported sporadically on the most extreme events, like hostage taking, attacks on warders and claims of "batter squads," but underneath these headline-making events there was a sort of daily war going on. The cons serving the longest terms, the lifers and no hopers, were gathered together on the edge of the cold North Sea and largely left to fester. The key was not actually thrown away (as many of the public would like it to have been) but it might as well have been. Relationships between captor and the caged were so far gone as to be seemingly irreparable. In a normal jail a wee kindness like a warder getting a prisoner an extra book or a wee treat of a chocolate biscuit or whatever was unremarkable. In Peterhead there were two sides in a war dug into psychological trenches staring at each other in mutual hatred and fear. Something had to give. And for a while the solution to the problem was the Special Unit down in Glasgow.

Psychologists and deep thinkers at the head of the prison service, and top civil servants in Edinburgh, realised that the missing ingredient in the whole mess up north was hope. They took the innovative step of doing something about it. The idea that a talent for art, be it sculpture or painting or writing, would solve any of Peterhead's problems had not been given any real thought up to this time. Indeed in the history of the Special Unit it is often remarked that educational facilities and such things as art classes were notably missing in the Peterhead prison regime. Requests for the provision of such facilities were refused.

If in many of Britain's prisons there was a new sense of growing humanitarianism and the belief a new way to treat offenders was needed, it was taking a long time to spread to the far North-East of Scotland. But eventually here, too, change was afoot. One of the main men behind the change of thinking was the late Ken Murray, a man from the north who was an experienced prison officer and who knew at first hand what the removal of hope could mean to a man in jail. Reports were written and seminars held. Good brains in the field of psychology were consulted. And eventually the decision to form a groundbreaking unit in Glasgow for a small number of the worst of the Peterhead troublemakers was taken. Until then these men had faced a future with no future. Now they were to be held in a group in a place where there was much more freedom than in a normal prison and where the hand-picked staff worked with the thinkers behind a much more liberal prison regime. Here the accent was on education and humanity rather than simply banging cell doors shut. In one touching story an ex-Peterhead con told of his surprise when a Special Unit warder handed him a pair of scissors to use in the completion of a task. Someone was trusting him with a potential weapon – amazing.

The Glasgow unit opened in 1973 and was a remarkable success till it withered slowly over the years and was closed in 1995 amid accusations of drug taking and cosy visits by females that went a lot further than chats across a table overseen by officers. But some of the more humane ideas that fuelled the Unit transferred successfully to other prisons on its closure. Whatever the controversies that still whirl around this world-famous penal experiment it is undeniable that in Hugh Collins and Jimmy Boyle, in particular, it uncovered men of real artistic talent who had spent years dismissed and condemned by society. The transformation of Jimmy Boyle from caged and dangerous animal into a favourite of the white-wine-sipping galleries of Edinburgh art circles is truly astounding. Told as a work of fiction you would have shaken your head in disbelief.

Some of the new thinking could be seen in the final days at Peterhead, where you could visit the education room – which has now an art teacher – and stroll the corridors admiring the work of the cons hanging from the cream-coloured walls that give the place the look and feel of a hospital in the areas away from the cell blocks. The standard is exceptionally high and anyone who gets a look at the paintings in particular is prompted to ponder the strange connection between crime and artistic ability. How is it that the man who can chib a criminal rival without a twinge of conscience can produce works of art that can be accurate, tender, eye-catching, and thought provoking? The "why" may be a mystery but the "how" is easy to explain. That comes from teachers with a love of art and the ability to see that under the skin of a hard man there can be something of value. Such people will be in demand in the glossy new classrooms of HMP Grampian.

14

FROM HATE FACTORY TO COLDitz!

The Peterhead sex offenders unit has made lots of headlines down the years, some in places far from Scotland's
North-East. There has been both criticism and spectacular
success for this remarkable specialised part of the Scottish
prison system. The pioneering treatment of rapists and
paedophiles made waves in many other penal systems.
Particularly in regard to the work of Alec Spencer, who
retired from the Scottish Prison Service in 2006 after
an impressive career in which he was responsible for
programmes involving, among other areas: addictions,
mental health, social inclusion and resettlement and treatment work with sex offenders. He then became Honorary
Professor in Criminology and Criminal Justice at Stirling
University. A glittering career for the man who had a spell
as governor of Peterhead from 1992–96.

A look at the backstory of the sex offenders unit is interesting. It took until 1954 before the gigantic breakwaters
creating the harbour were fully completed. All the work
down the years on this project was hugely worthwhile.
Maritime engineering experts point out that not only did

it fulfil its original task of saving lives of fishermen and whalers but when the oil boom came in the 1970s it was a huge advantage to the town. One expert wrote in 1984 that the breakwaters created an excellent entry to the lagoon that is Peterhead Bay and that "at no time has a fishing boat failed to make this harbour of refuge under storm conditions, and it is hoped that no one will change this situation by altering the breakwaters at the entrance."

The best way to view the massive works is from the air, where you see clearly how the long fingers of rock march out from the shore to create the huge deep-water harbour of today. Those who toiled in the Admiralty yard and in the quarries could take back to their homes in the Central Belt, if they survived to taste freedom, the knowledge that they had contributed to a great humanitarian and engineering project. Mind you, human nature being what it is, I doubt if the villains who worked on the breakwaters and broke stone in the quarries ever thought very much on its value to society. They just wanted to get out.

The final completing of the breakwaters meant big changes at the prison as the work in the quarry and the Admiralty yard was phased out. In 1959 around twenty acres were added to the original area of the prison. The big idea was to use this land as an "industrial area" to provide work for prisoners who now no longer laboured in primitive fashion breaking stone in Stirling Hill quarry. The prisoners were not the only folk put out of work by the completion of the harbour. The divers in their old-fashioned brass helmets, tethered to a pump supplying oxygen, who laboured underwater for years helping to align the granite blocks of the breakwater were also out of a job, at least in Peterhead. These guys, when dressed for a day underwater, looked as if they would be more at home as pearl fishers rather than descending into the cold North Sea. Though they are now part of nautical history as sub aqua divers, the act of carrying air in cylinders on their backs now rules the undersea working world – especially round the rigs out in the North Sea just over the horizon from the harbour. In the Peterhead archives there is a fine picture of the final group of divers who worked on the breakwater. Sad to think that those iconic old helmets are a thing of the past, the brass polished and shiny as they gaze out at you from antique shops or museum cases.

The completion of the Harbour of Refuge meant that Peterhead took on the role of an ordinary prison. It became home to prisoners serving more than eighteen months who were deemed inappropriate to be sent to a training prison. This meant that in the 1970s and '80s the jail was filled with difficult and recalcitrant prisoners. The good boys just intent on a quiet life, keeping their heads down and doing their time were sent elsewhere. The seeds of the major riots and hostage taking chronicled earlier in this book had been well and truly sown. Already there were intermittent calls for the closure of the prison – though it lasted around another thirty years. Prisoners took every chance they could to complain that the regime was violent and bruising. This was the heyday of The Hate Factory.

In 1979 a researcher at Stirling University, Russell Dobash, visited and in his report he said, "I was shocked by the austere environment. I have been in every other Scottish prison and the conditions in Peterhead are exceptional in the negative sense, far beyond what one would have expected. There is an urgent need for a change at Peterhead, in fact it should be considered whether it should still operate as a prison in this day and age . . . I don't know if it can be improved without knocking the place down."

Part of the problem was poor cells and generally accommodation that was not fit for purpose. Some of the cells were so small they were known as "iron lungs." These were the ones that had been designed originally to hold a hammock rather than a bed. The remoteness of the prison from the Central Belt, which is where most of the inmates came from, was another disadvantage. This, of course, removed many prisoners from the civilising influence of regular family visits. Or at least made them more infrequent than would otherwise have been the case. It was a major drawback which in time was to contribute to the closing of the sex offenders unit. A list of the complaints about the place was drawn up around this time. It makes disturbing reading:

- Facilities for visits were poor.
- Education facilities were limited.
- Hygiene was considered deplorable: "Only two wash hand basins and two showers for forty men."
- Prisoners did not receive regular and frequent changes of clothing, particularly underwear and bedding.
- Prisoners were still slopping out.
- Heating, ventilation and lighting in cells was considered poor.

Though the prison housed difficult prisoners there were also a number of prisoners who required protection. This was because they had fallen foul of one group of prisoners or another – the feuding "teams" of prisoners. Or because of the nature of their crimes such as paedophilia, rape, etc. The annexe of B Hall, which was separated from the main

B Hall by a partition, was used to house up to twenty-one such prisoners.

This was perhaps the start of the sex offenders unit. In the late 1980s when the prison service, with some help from the SAS, had got some semblance of real control of the place, it was decided to disperse many of the prisoners who had not been involved in the riots to other prisons such as Shotts, Perth and Glenochil. The hardcore were left behind and kept in their own cells on a "lock-down" basis. This was the era of officers in body armour managing the violent cons. The moving of some of the less nasty specimens in Peterhead to other jails meant that space had to be found for them and this meant sending some cons who were not vicious chip-on-their-shoulder hard men north. This changed the balance of life in The Hate Factory, diluting the aggro between groups. One effect was that vulnerable prisoners were able to move around the prison more freely as the cons who would most likely attack them were safely locked up. This allowed these prisoners to get involved in such tasks as cleaning and cooking.

But soon new arrangements meant that the prisoners who needed special protection were transferred to C Hall and there they were joined by forty prisoners who had been under protection in other prisons. Some short-term low-risk prisoners were also transferred from Aberdeen prison. This resulted in the difficult prisoners being held in four different locations in the prison. The most dangerous and difficult – the men judged by the prison authorities to be the most serious threat to staff – were held on the ground flat of B Hall. These were the men held under Rule 36, the hardest haters in The Hate Factory, the men out for revenge on society in general and prison staff in particular.

The daily strain of contact with men who were considered caged and dangerous "animals" cannot be underestimated and was no doubt a factor in the suicide of some prison officers who broke under the stress of working in such a jail.

A remaining group of problem prisoners was held on the two bottom flats of D Hall. They, unlike the Rule 36 men, were allowed to associate in pairs. The remaining two groups were held in the bottom flats of A and E Halls. At the same time as these constrictive and confrontational regimes were running the normal prison regime was available to vulnerable prisoners.

The last twenty-five years or so were a nightmare of uncertainty for the staff. There was abroad the feeling that the establishment had outstayed its usefulness and that it should close. Everyone who worked in the prison from the most humble new start officer to the top brass was concerned about the future. And the local community which had learned to live with a tough jail almost in the centre of town was also worried. The jail brought many financial benefits to the area, benefits that some estimates put as valuable as ten million pounds. There was a lot to play for.

As early as November 1991 senior staff appealed for an end to the uncertainty that surrounded the future of the prison since "the Troubles," as the riots and unrest of the 1970s and '80s were now called. There was no clear answer to the uncertainty of the long-term future, but a decision was taken to concentrate sex offenders in Peterhead. This was formally announced by the Chief Executive of the Scottish Prison Service in January 1992. In June of the same year the Chief Inspector of Prisons delivered a measure of criticism of the regimes faced by what was called the "difficult prisoner" group. However, he remarked favourably on the changes to the regime for vulnerable prisoners and remarked that it was superior to anything found elsewhere in the system.

But it was early days in the work of the sex offenders unit and the Chief Inspector noted that the management of the prisoners in it had hardly advanced beyond the embryonic stage in Scotland in terms of penal policy. He gave his support to the work envisaged for the development of the treatment of sex offenders in the prison and before the year was out classes and discussion groups for staff had started. An impressive array of experts in social work were at the prison helping get the unit off the ground. Among the experts was Canadian Professor Bill Marshall and the unit gradually evolved into something of a world leader in the field and attracted attention worldwide.

In 1992 Alec Spencer, at the time Director of Rehabilitation and Care for the Scottish Prison Service, chaired a group examining the whole area of treatment for sexual offenders. Among the other experts involved was Stuart Campbell. Stuart was Peterhead's Prisoner Programme Manager and was to go on to become Deputy Governor and one of the senior staff in charge in 2013 as the jail ran down towards final closure.

Mike Hebden, the governor himself, had a major job on his hands as the replacement prison HMP Grampian was being planned and built and he would be working there after its opening. To free him up for his new role, Audrey Mooney was appointed governor for the last few months in the old jail.

The group produced an impressive document: The Spencer Report. The big argument was one that had

180

bedevilled prison services in many countries. Should sex offenders be held and attempts to rehabilitate them made in a large "monoculture" establishment or in smaller units in mainstream prisons? Many of the same arguments surfaced in the case of the Barlinnie Special Unit. It is interesting that The Spencer Report came down strongly on one side: "Having examined the range of options we have concluded that the best environment for the delivery of programmes to address sexual offending is that to be found in a 'single-purpose' prison for Adult Male Sex Offenders. As well as optimising resources and treatment efficiency, it has a culture which is supportive of staff, prisoners and visitors."

The Spencer Report had much to say as well about the conditions in such a single-purpose unit – naturally, decent sanitation (no slopping out) was high on the agenda but also the provision of adequate rooms for group work, interviews, case conferences, etc. Attention was also to be paid to good visiting areas, seminar facilities and a resource library. Most of this was notably absent from Peterhead, which despite its physical disadvantage was to continue for around another twenty years and achieve much success and admiration from other people working in the field. That says a lot about the dedication and ability of the folk who took on the largely thankless double task of protecting the public from a most dangerous type of criminal and attempting some degree of rehabilitation.

It is interesting that though the Spencer Report did advocate a "single-use" prison for sex offenders it also noted some alternative arguments. It advocated the importance of Throughcare, of which contacts with communities and families are a crucial part. On this issue it said, "Thus the optimal location is one which is as close to home areas of offenders as can be organised within the requirement to provide a 'single-purpose' prison."

The one-time Chief Inspector of Prisons, Clive Fair-weather, was another to want the unit retained in full in Peterhead. As was the North-East MP Alex Salmond, Scotland's current First Minster, though to be fair to him his major concern was probably to maintain a large "ordinary" prison in the area for economic reasons. The prison was a major employer in the area and there were all sorts of spin-off benefits to the community: the provision of fresh food, etc. One student of the penal system told me that "the First Minister's designation of Peterhead as 'the jewel in the crown of the Scottish prison service' overstated the case somewhat!" Cynics using social media filled large areas of cyber space commenting on the value of the prison in jobs and cash to the folk of Banff and Buchan. No harm in fighting hard for your constituents, I would say, and there is no doubt that Alex Salmond did that.

As it happens, a new single-use prison for sex offenders was never built, largely because it could not be visitor-friendly and suitable for Throughcare. So with the closure of Peterhead imminent the convicts in its special unit were dispersed to other prisons. But the good work done in Peterhead and the expertise built up will not be wasted but put to good use in other establishments. It is also interesting to note that with regard to dispersal strategy of sex offenders, England and Wales rejected the concentration policy in favour of dispersal as long ago as the 1960s.

Alex Spencer's intellectual "take" on what went on in the institution during and after his time would, however, you suspect, not always chime with the opinions of the general public. A case in point would be the affair of the trendy pillows! This storm in a sewing basket broke out in 2010 when the *Daily Record* ran an exclusive headlined: "Charity Pays Pervert Prisoners £60 for Sewing Cushions." It seems that prisoners in the sex offenders unit were "cashing in" on the demand for trendy cushions and earning £60 a pop for cushions and such like that were sold by an organisation called Fine Cell Work for around £150 a time.

Embroidery experts from Fine Cell Work were said to travel to prisons in Scotland and England to hold specialist workshops. It was certainly all rather different from the '70s when, as mentioned earlier in this book, the Glasgow Godfather and his cronies behind bars made soft toys for the world-famous Sick Children's Hospital in Glasgow. Walter Norval and his mates bought the cloth and stuffing from their own prison wages. It was not a money-making operation. This minor row over the pillows is an indication that sometimes what went on in the sex offenders unit went a tad too far for the man and woman in the street: witness the anger in the Twitter-sphere when the pillow scheme became public. It was all a bit reminiscent of the furore created by the teaching of creative writing, painting and sculpture in the old Barlinnie Special Unit. Some outside the bars have no stomach for any ploy, however well meaning, that equates with what they call a cushy life inside a prison, especially a sex offenders unit.

But what was it really like in the place that held paedophiles, serial killers and rapists? A row over a few fancy cushions is swatted into insignificance by the reality. In its final days the unit was highly praised for its work but it had a barbaric predecessor – "the digger," as the original Peterhead segregation unit was called. Prisons throughout the world have similar places. In American jails it would be "the hole." It is remarkable that in the closing years of the twentieth century such places still existed. In less enlightened times troublemakers in prisons were more likely to be literally thrown into a hole in the ground and left to rot rather that receive counselling or cognitive behavioural therapy. Dirty protests, attacks on warders and disruptive behaviour meant long months in solitary or deep in the darkness of the digger. Those prisoners cast into such pits became dangerous men and the public got a hint of it in the 1980s with those stories of warders in full riot gear standing by whenever the cell doors were opened.

But eventually as the years passed there was a gradual change in society's attitude to what was happening in such places. The prison service itself changed and slowly more emphasis was put on treating the psychological problems of sex offenders in addition to making sure the public was safe from their vile crimes. In the mainstream parts of prisons, there was also a change of attitude. Schemes like "training for freedom" evolved and prison officers became more interested and involved with their charges rather than being mere jailers. The battle to stop reoffending will never be complete but at least these days things are inching in the right direction. It is a healthy change.

What went on in the digger in the early days would have been red meat for any horror film director. The place smelled of violence and hatred. It was all rather different in the final days of the sex offenders unit, but it was still no place for the faint-hearted to visit. A perceptive and sad insight into the atmosphere in the unit was told to me by one of Scotland's top columnists and radio and TV broadcasters, Ruth Wishart. Ruth has long had an interest in the penal system and in particular the effect on offenders' families and the difficulties encountered by them with prison-visiting regimes. Indeed she has campaigned to help get better access for relatives and more understanding for them from the public. Here is how she told me of her visit to the Unit in Peterhead:

"I had written about the sex offenders unit in Peterhead prison at various points, and interviewed academics, social workers and others about the likelihood of successful treatment, the dangers of reoffending, and the problems posed post-release in terms of neighbourhood protests. But then print journalism with tricky subjects is relatively easy. You control and edit what appears and you select the cast list according to the points you want to get over. However, when I was working as a daily broadcaster for BBC Radio Scotland, it was suggested that a programme from the pioneering sex offenders unit might make compelling listening, and that raised a whole raft of more difficult issues – not the least of which was getting the Scottish Prison Service to agree.

"In the event they were extremely helpful. They knew we weren't in the business of sensationalising the subject; we'd already agreed to anonymity for the prisoners concerned, and, as it was a pre-record, there was the possibility of editing out anything problematical.

"We also had agreement from the many professionals across different specialisms who regularly worked with the men in the unit in terms of unravelling their motivation, assessing their personalities, and working to make them accept and confront the fact that their behaviour was completely beyond the pale – because it's dispiritingly usual for many such men to insist that the people they abuse, especially children, were willing co-conspirators, to whom they were merely offering love.

185

"So far, so good. I went up to Peterhead with a producer and sound engineer and talked through the practicalities of where we would record and how many men would take part. There were no particular restrictions placed on what we could ask, only the reasonable insistence that nothing we said could in any way identify the victims.

"Then, with all systems go, word came through to us that the men themselves had changed their minds. They didn't want to take part anymore. Without their agreement we had no programme. I asked the prison authorities if I could talk to them as a group and they agreed.

"As has so often been said before, the men gathered round me in the room set aside for recording looked like the kind of men you might meet in the supermarket queue. A seemingly perfectly normal cross-section in terms of age, shape and social background. Most were there because they had groomed and abused children. One of the younger ones was in the unit because of his persistently violent behaviour to his partner. Some had a record of violently abusing women.

"I spent twenty minutes trying to reassure these guys that they would not be demonised or identified, that we were trying to help the public understand why they did what they did. How they themselves felt about it. Whether or not they thought the unit would change the way they behaved were they to be released.

"What clinched the deal was my promise that all of them would be given totally different names, and that these would be written on a placard and attached to their chests so that we would all know who was "John" and who was "Derek" when we started to have a real conversation for the recording. What we hadn't factored in was that while all the men sitting in a circle could readily see everyone else's identity card they couldn't, of course, see their own. And most of the time, they seemed to forget their recently acquired first name. So I would say something like, 'Tell me, Bill, about the first time you felt sexual thoughts about a child,' and 'Bill' would studiously ignore me because he was Frank. But we got there in the end, although it was a quite surreal experience. You sit there looking as these men who respond politely and seem entirely unthreatening in every way, and you have to remind yourself that in some cases they are very dangerous people indeed. I remember, for instance, asking one man where and how he selected children to groom. He didn't have to, he mumbled. And I realised that was because his chosen victims were his own family – as is so often the case. Stranger danger is much less common than the threats within a child's own family circle.

"Normally when you do these outside broadcasts on location you go off afterwards for a meal and a few drinks and unwind with a few laughs. This one proved a bit different. There didn't, in the event, seem very much to laugh about."

This insight into the world of the sex offender is unsettling, a feeling that affects many visitors to the unit. Long after you have returned to the outside and normality it is hard to get the place out of your mind. The cause is the curious contrasts in life in such a place. On the surface there is the down-to-earth atmosphere of cups of tea and custard creams, it could be a hospital waiting room or more likely an open prison. But all the time in your mind is the disturbing knowledge of the stark reality of the vile crimes of the inmates and the necessity for high-level security.

Holyrood Magazine, edited by Mandy Rhodes, is Scotland's fortnightly political and current affairs magazine that keeps the country's movers and shakers informed about happenings on their patch. In 2010 it contained a remarkable and fascinating insight into the unit. It is a piece worth reading:

It is disarmingly childlike, the small single bed with its Manchester United duvet cover and PlayStation controller on the pillow. A television sits in the corner surrounded by bottles of soft drink. But this is no young child's room. On the desk there's an exercise book containing small neat rows and columns of figures with occasional annotations. It's a record of income and expenditure. The sums are pathetically small, the few pounds spent on the juice and chocolate, toothpaste, other sundries. And the tables stretch back not just weeks and months, but years. Into the previous century.

This is the cell of a sex offender at HMP Peterhead prison. The man who lives inside it has committed a terrible offence, been tried and convicted and is now serving a very long sentence. Yet as the cell shows, he eats and washes and sleeps, just like the rest of us. He follows a football team. He likes to relax by playing video games. He's careful with his money.

On the surface, he's just like you and me.

And one day he will be released back into society. That is what makes him so complex and dangerous.

Pamela Macdougall leads one of the psychology teams at Peterhead. An attractive young woman, she seems like a character from a thriller brought to life.

The prison itself has a similar quality, an imposing nineteenth-century facility set on a headland that juts out in to the swelling grey North Sea.

A key part of the rehabilitation work the inmates undergo – and all 306 men currently housed at Peterhead have chosen to take part in the specialised sex offender treatment programme; those who refuse to do so serving their sentences in HMP Dumfries – involves discussing their offending behaviour in group situations overseen by a trained professional like Macdougall.

"Sitting in group when you hear them going through their offending behaviour, I think before you go into the group room, you have read their files and you've read the indictment and what they've done and I think it really hits home that they're the person sitting there right in front of you.

"To start with, that was a real initial shock factor but I have been here so long I have become accustomed to it. But when you hear some of them disclosing some of the things they've done that haven't been reported before, it has real shock value, as does the really violent and sadistic crime.

"They are the ones that really hit home," she says.

Macdougall then goes on to describe the tortuous paradox at the heart of dealing with sex offenders. Being a trained professional, she cannot subscribe to the tabloid notion that the men she works with are evil by nature, or somehow less than human, beasts. But she does admit that some do seem to be beyond treatment, at least in the time she has with them.

"I wouldn't necessarily say that I view them as being born bad, I would say they enjoy their offending behaviour so much they don't want to change. I have come across a handful that are like that. They are a minority. It is just because they enjoyed what they were doing so

189

much and that is a hard one to deal with, especially when you know they are going to be released.

"I had a recent example at the end of last year and I knew the guy was going and I could pretty much have said he would reoffend. He was in for sexually assaulting his aunt and when I was interviewing him he was disclosing all this other offending behaviour and when he was away to be released I did a report on it and I could have put money on it that he would reoffend but there was nothing we could do because it was his sentence expiry date.

"He ended up committing another offence and he's actually waiting to be charged with it. If they really want to, they are going to continue to do it."

And that is what is so troubling about walking around Peterhead. Some of these men committed horrendous crimes, enjoyed doing it and would do it again, given a chance. Being given the guided tour by Governor Mike Hebden, the place is visibly different from other prisons. For a start, the population is noticeably older. This reflects the nature of many sex offenders, who are often not caught for many years.

In addition, the average age has been pushed up by the increase in convictions for what is termed historical abuse – offences committed years, even decades ago, but only prosecuted recently, meaning the offenders are often well into middle age, or even elderly, when incarcerated. [*It is interesting that now in the twenty-first century and the crimes of such as Jimmy Savile and Stuart Hall have been exposed that trend has increased remarkably.*]

The other thing you notice is that Peterhead is much quieter than other prisons. Where places like Barlinnie sound more like a football match with continual shouting and announcements over the Tannoy, Peterhead is almost silent. Hebden says this is borne out in the wider atmosphere of the jail. Violent incidents, attacks on staff and incidents between prisoners are rare, far lower than in other jails. There is little drug use and no gang culture. But this does not mean the prisoners are benign. Far from it. It is just that instead of using physical force to gain advantage, they use their brains. Just as the majority of sex offenders will plot and manipulate to create the situations in which they can commit their crimes and then use similar tactics to keep their victims from speaking out, so they use similar tactics once locked up.

A key concern for staff is that prisoners will learn what they are expected to say while undergoing the treatment programme and make every effort to appear to be complying and 'getting better' in order to hasten their release date so they can offend again.

"There is definitely that," says Macdougall. "They learn the group language and what they are 'supposed' to be saying and what we try and do is use other sources to try and see if what they are saying is true and if their behaviour actually is changing or whether there is something else going on there."

That's where an officer like Dale Galley comes in. Galley helps facilitate group sessions but also ensures that prisoners' behaviour is constantly monitored and cross-referenced.

"It's very difficult to keep an act up 24/7," he says. "They might learn what they think we want to hear and they will say, 'I have changed, I've realised this about myself,' but then you can say back to them, 'Well, in the halls you've been seen engaging in some pretty questionable behaviour with some of the other guys,' you can challenge that, tell them they are only kidding themselves."

To aid this, all group sessions are taped by a discreet CCTV camera. Galley says the treatment programme – which has been remodelled and will be rolled out in a new modular form in coming months that allows for inmates to give greater focus to certain areas – is based on a cognitive behaviour therapy model.

"It is about getting them to think through the circumstances that led up to their offending, of why they committed that offence. Did you really 'subconsciously' walk past that school every day or was it something more than that, something a bit more conscious than you're admitting?" he says.

The vast majority of offenders first attempt to deny what they did, then they try and blame the victim and finally, once they have accepted their guilt, attempt to minimise the impact of their crime. The challenge for people like Galley and Macdougall is to continue that path to a point where the offender recognises not only that they did commit a horrific offence that has damaged the victim's life, often irreparably, but to learn why they did it and develop strategies to prevent them from reoffending when they are released, because apart from eleven men on Orders of Lifelong Restriction, every single inmate in Peterhead will be released back into the community at some point.

I meet some prisoners briefly while walking through the halls with Hebden. Unlike in normal prisons where inmates are often quick to engage with a visiting journalist, often with some banter, these men are more reserved, clearly assessing the situation, ensuring they don't say the wrong thing in front of the Governor. The conversation is brief and reveals little yet still manages to be deeply unsettling. It sounds like a terrible cliché, but I can actively sense the three men's eyes on my back as I walk out of the cell where they have been smoking and watching television prior to our arrival.

Change is afoot at the prison. Peterhead as a dedicated facility for sex offenders is closing and the building will be knocked down, a new one built and its capacity and catchment merged with Craiginches prison in Aberdeen to become HMP Grampian. And as Hebden, a man who started his career in the prison service in the days when Peterhead housed the nation's toughest and most disruptive inmates says with dry understatement, "It was a very mentally and physically challenging place to work." He also notes that both HMP Edinburgh and Barlinnie in Glasgow already house sex offenders serving short-term sentences of four years or less, while Polmont houses young offenders convicted of sex offences.

"People are under the impression that Peterhead is the only sex-offender site and that is not the case and hasn't been for some time. It is the main sex-offenders site for long-term sex offenders. There are roughly 600 sex offenders in the system at any time, it varies, and half of them would be here. We're the largest site but not the only site," he says.

Hebden acknowledges the concern that altering what had previously been considered a world-leading practice – that of housing sex offenders in a dedicated site run like a mainstream jail with a clear focus on treatment – comes with some risks: "It is a concern that has been raised in a number of forums previously and it would have been a concern perhaps five or six years ago but because of the success that Peterhead has had in managing sex offenders, we have taken that best practice and developed it at other sites.

"So we have a level of expertise and experience in working with sex offenders and treating sex offenders across the estate now. It isn't just a one-stop shop. We are far more comfortable that the risk can be managed. There is still a risk with the movement of prisoners regardless of type or offence.

"The main risk for us is a drop in the service provided, a cut off whereby when we cut off here it doesn't start somewhere else. Our plans need to make sure that as we run down we run up so that at no point is the safety of the public put at risk by the failure of us to treat or securely contain and manage the risk of convicted sex offenders and we are well aware of that. I have no concerns about that."

He continues: "This move has been hanging over our heads since about 2000 when it was initially mooted that the prison would close. At that point, sex offenders were very much against [it] because they feared being put back into a mainstream setting so they really want to stay here because of the quality of life here – it is a mainstream prison for sex offenders, they don't have separate regimes, they don't have to go to separate locations, separate work sheds, their visitors aren't under the same pressure they would be. They feared they would lose a lot.

"But as an organisation we have matured a lot since then in the management of sex offenders and we don't have

194

the same issues at Edinburgh and Barlinnie and Polmont we used to have in the way in which sex offenders are perceived. The fear of going somewhere else and being marginalised or victimised is greatly reduced.

"They go there for visits occasionally, they have come to us from there once they are sentenced. I think they know and trust the SPS to ensure, regardless of where they are, they will receive appropriate treatment and will be safe."

This is the hallmark of the staff at Peterhead. In a society where sex offenders, especially those who commit crimes against children, are widely held to be the lowest of the low, they conduct themselves with ultimate profession-alism at all times.

I ask Macdougall if she has had any disturbing expe-riences in her time working with these men and she recounts a truly unpleasant anecdote: "In one of my experiences in group, a guy actually committed a sexual offence while I was in group. That was directed at me, he was masturbating in his pocket.

'It was one of those moments where because I've worked here for so long I've always thought I can deal with absolutely anything and I know how to deal with anything but I felt a bit frozen. The guy had committed really violent offences as well and I was a bit like, I'm not really sure how to challenge this. That was the first time I've ever felt like, "What on Earth do I do?" But she stresses this was the only time an incident of that nature occurred and then describes the men in a way most observers would struggle to comprehend but reflects the reality of these people, that for all the hideous crimes they have committed, they are still indeed human beings and that our challenge as a society is to balance their crimes against that innate reality.

She says: "I have built a good relationship with quite a lot of the guys I have worked with. I get to see the other side of them other than their offending, I get to see the good side, the ones with great personalities, really funny. It is those little elements that people wouldn't really pick up on and that I see."

That sort of view of life in a sex offenders unit is not something that the average Scot samples at first hand. The population at large depends on newspaper accounts and TV and radio documentaries for their understanding of what goes on behind bars in the prison service from sex offender units to mainstream prisons and low security prisons and halfway houses. Not surprisingly, the grim place that is Peterhead has down the years fascinated newspapers both broadsheet and tabloid. It is interesting that perceptive writers like Ruth Wishart and Mandy Rhodes got plenty of space in papers such as *The Scotsman* and *The Herald* to give thinking readers real insight into what was going on behind the high walls of the prison.

News editors and feature editors seem to have a predilection to send their top women reporters to look at life in the toughest of units. Maggie Barry of the *Mirror* group is another who visited the sex offenders unit and she had an interesting interview with Audrey Mooney, the first woman governor in the UK of a specialist unit for sex offenders. Described as "slight, slim and blonde with piercing blue eyes" she told Maggie of the difference between a mainstream prison and a specialist sex unit: "It's a different environment completely. In a normal prison the population moves very quickly and there are a lot of issues around drugs and mental health. You are always aware of violence and when it erupts it erupts quickly, usually in reaction to something. In a sex offenders unit you have a stable population serving long sentences who are more compliant." [*Some are terrified of being put into the normal prison population where revulsion at their crimes makes them a target: many a prisoner would be delighted to take the chance to attack what they call a "beast."*] Audrey went on to talk about the eerie, indeed, creepy atmosphere. The men inside these units are a different breed – on the outside they groomed and stalked their victims. Inside, for the most part their attitude has not changed. "Everything that happens is premeditated. It is subtle and manipulative."

Those who worked in the sex offenders unit are well aware of the danger, though it is comforting to note that there were few serious incidents and nothing to compare with the ordeal of officers taken hostage in the dark days of the '80s. But there were potentially dangerous incidents, perhaps the worst happening in spring 2011, not all that long before the dispersal of the criminals held in the Special Unit to other establishments.

An officer, a woman in her forties, suffered attempted rape at knifepoint. She screamed in terror as an inmate tried to pull her trousers down. She had been working alone in a room normally used for group activities when she heard a noise and was grabbed from behind and some sort of knife held at her throat and told to keep quiet. Fortunately her screaming quickly attracted other officers who jostled the attacker to the ground and locked him in a cell before he was interviewed by the police. Not surprisingly, the officer was devastated by the attack and had to take time off work.

It was a fairly uncommon incident but a real reminder of the dangers of working in such a place.

Maggie Barry's report also raised an interesting issue. In a normal prison no one is shocked by a page three "stunnah" blue-tacked to the wall. Most governors are not too happy about it but a blind eye can sometimes be useful. But in a sex offenders unit? The walls of the six foot by twelve cells are officially allowed to be decorated by the inmates. But where do you draw the line? Should a paedophile have pictures of young female relatives on the wall? I suppose the best you can do is deal with it on a case by case basis, but it is an on-going concern. Like most of what goes on in a sex offenders unit, there is no easy answer.

The contribution of such insightful journalism as that from Ruth, Mandy and Maggie to prison reform cannot be underestimated. With notable and praiseworthy exceptions, most of this analysis occurs in the broadsheet press. The role of the tabloids is a rather different matter and they can on occasion create myths on prison life in the minds of the readers and then pander to the perceptions partly caused by their own sensationalist reporting.

A few years ago one of Scotland's most respected prison governors told me of his frustration at the way some newspapers portray prison life. An example he gave was the constant repetition of the use of the phrase "flat-screen TVs" whenever conditions in a jail are discussed in the tabloid press. The phrase conjures up visions of loafers, beer in hand, lounging on leather sofas before forty-inch screens watching old movies or the latest sports events. The reality is different – the sets are small-screen and often shared between several cons at least. There are constant arguments about what to watch and the company is not attractive to the fastidious. What tends to be ignored is the fact that various studies have shown that allowing controlled TV watching in prison is of therapeutic value in calming down caged men, many of whom can't read or take solace in a book or educate themselves.

It is also a window on the world outside the bars. In the old days before TV and radio prisoners could leave a jail after years and enter a world very unlike the way it was when they were sent down. You think of the character Books in that fine prison drama *The Shawshank Redemption* – released after years, he simply can't face the pace of modern life and commits suicide. Anything, even dire soap operas, is better than to be left staring at the wall hour after hour with nothing to think about other than jealously wondering what your mates are up to on the outside. That can build up resentment that leads to attacks on prison officers and, occasionally, contributes to full-blown riots in which many people get hurt. The level of violence in prison has fallen with the introduction of TVs.

My governor friend also played a master card with a smile – in the twenty-first century even the tiniest of TVs is flat-screen! Think smart-phone-size, not fifty-inch wall-mounted entertainment systems when you are discussing TV in the nation's nicks. More broadly, it has to be admitted that much of the broadsheet press is preaching to the converted, the liberal elite, and that the tabloids are spreading the word about crime and punishment, retribution or reform, to the people most likely to be involved themselves.

The popular press never misses an opportunity to keep their readers abreast of what is happening to headline cons like serial killer Peter Tobin, who flits around the prison system and has served much time in Peterhead. At the time

199

of their trials the doings of such as Tobin and others, who affront and fascinate in almost equal degree, fill page after page. Those who compile the reports in the tabloids have little use for a thesaurus – the cynic might say just choose an adjective from a ready collection such as evil, monster, beast, vile, depraved, caged, or whatever and off you go. But in their own way the tabloids play a role in the evolution of the prison service. Their reporters are a vital link between the men and women behind bars and their families, and their jailers and society in general. There should be no secrecy about what goes on in prisons. A classic example is capital punishment. Detailed reports of the horror of deliberately killing a human being contributed greatly to the clamour that led to its abolition. To be "hung by the neck until you are dead" is easy and quick to say – to read in detail the grim process of an execution and its effect on those who participate and witness the calculated and deliberate killing of a human being is another matter. Had the death penalty been conducted in total secrecy it probably would be with us today as a blemish on a civilised society.

Pin-ups on cell walls and rows over cosy cushions are only some of the controversies that are generated by happenings in jails such as Barlinnie and Peterhead. The media ferrets out anything at all unusual, such as secret booze brewing factories or drugs smuggled into cells. You can't hide from a good investigative reporter. Ask any governor! And those "inside" stories can spark what you might call reading rage among the punters who buy the tabloids. That little tale of the money earned sewing cushions was one example – even more annoying to the public at large was the story that, for a time, changed the nickname of Peterhead, from The Hate Factory to COLDitz.

It happened a few years ago and at the centre of the row was sex pervert Tobin, the killer of two teenagers, Vicky Hamilton and Dinah McNicol, and a Polish student in Glasgow called Angelika Kluk. You could not make it up, as they say, but Tobin and some mates were complaining that it was too cold in the jail and that the heating was turned off too early in the spring and back on too late in the autumn. Tobin is an expert in complaining – in almost every nick he is sent to he would complain about something or other and he is an expert at faking illness to gain attention and trips from jail to court. He took any and every chance to moan about his treatment. But, by any standards, for a prisoner to complain it is cold in Peterhead takes some hard neck. Remember back in the early days the governor would not even let you wrap your blanket round you when not in bed. The complete lack of shame shown by Tobin also surfaced when in jail in England when he whined he wanted a transfer to a Scottish nick since he was "lonely." That is hard to beat as a prison complaint.

Ask any old lag about his time in the jail "up north" and he will mention the gales howling in from the North Sea in storms that often began in the frozen wastes of northern Russia and Greenland before sweeping south to Scotland. The sort of guys that Walter Norval is wont to call "proper" cons took the freezing conditions as par for the course, as a golfer might say. And the locals, including those who still fish the wild waters nearby, also took it as a fact of life in such a place. But here in the twenty-first century the papers were telling the citizenry that the most evil of the evil men held in the local jail were complaining about central heating. This little story generated a lot of heat, appropriately, locally. And zero sympathy.

Before the decision was taken to disperse the sex offenders to other units after HMP Grampian opens, the place was home to many of the worst offenders behind bars in Scotland. It is interesting to reflect that not so long ago many of the inmates could have ended their life on the gallows rather than be treated in a special unit. As well as in its final days holding Peter Tobin, the sex offenders unit also held a villain called William Beggs, who was convicted of killing an Ayrshire teenager after a Christmas night out in Kilmarnock. Beggs dismembered his victim, leaving body parts in Loch Lomond and his head in the sea off Troon, hence his tag in the press – The Limbs in the Loch Killer. There seemed to be over-representation of Ayrshire in the newspaper crime world for a while. In addition to Beggs, Charles O'Neill, who preyed on young boys in Skelmorlie and Irvine, was held in Peterhead. Other infamous names in the unit included Robert Foyle and Lee Barrass, who killed a *Big Issue* seller and committed a sex act over her body. Newspaper stushies on how these villains were treated made regular headlines and outraged members of the public. Typical was a story that Beggs of all people had been accepted on a joinery course in the jail. The outrage in this case has some serious validity – Beggs has had experience with saws.

Apart from butchery, Beggs had another area of expertise when in jail. He became a notorious jailhouse lawyer who eases the pain of confinement by bombarding the authorities with legal claims and advising cons on appeals and compensation claims. There is a slight echo of another famous jailhouse lawyer – Johnny Ramensky, whose crimes, it must be said, were as of nothing compared to that of Beggs. There is also a similarity to the Great Escaper's prison campaigns for better medical treatment in a recent spat Beggs has had with the authorities. The killer angered the establishment with claims in a prison magazine that the authorities had not acted with suitable speed in the case of an elderly paedophile who had complained of being ill. The prison service responded: "We have well qualified medical staff in all prisons who will provide expert care." Despite what might have happened back in the '30s, no one could argue that prisoners today do not get that expert care.

Another recent row was over the sort of DVDs inmates were allowed to watch. The newspaper outrage in this case was over the supply of films featuring murder and violence. The prison PR people are always on the back foot when such issues get into the papers and generally rely on saying they "do not comment on individual prisoners." The DVD story makes regular return appearances in the papers. But it is hard to get a DVD today that will not contain something that someone somewhere will complain about. And watching DVDs in controlled circumstances is, like TV itself, a possibly calming influence.

Another resident of Peterhead was Robert Black the infamous child killer. In 2012 in a Channel 5 TV series *Killers Behind Bars* Professor David Williams says he believes Black may be the most prolific child killer in British criminal history. Black had already been convicted of four murders. Professor Williams said, "I am convinced this is just the tip of the iceberg." The eminent criminologist had met a Scottish policeman, DCI Andrew Watt, who had investigated the murder of one of Black's victims. Similarities to unsolved child murders were noted. He also studied interviews with Black recorded in Peterhead. In the programme Professor

Williams called for a series of unsolved child murder cases to be reopened.

The enormity of the crimes committed by such men as those shows the significance of the unit that went from a low-key start to end up being named as a "centre of excellence" in dealing with sex offenders. To receive such an accolade for containing and attempting to treat such dangerous deviants was a remarkable achievement and a tribute to the staff. But it is dispiriting to note that the first transfer of sex offenders to Glenochil in Clackmannanshire met with criticism in some quarters, as it raised that old prison bogey: overcrowding. The problem was highlighted in a report by HM Chief Inspector of Prisons Brigadier Hugh Munro late in 2010. He said that the impact of the transfer of sex offenders from Peterhead (to Glenochil) had been "considerable." His report stated: "There is very strict segregation of these prisoners from others within the regime and this causes restrictions, particularly in terms of access to activities and programmes.

"Inevitably each of the two different populations perceives that they have lost out. Overcrowding has become more acute and the instances of 'doubled-up' single cells in Harviestoun Hall caused a disproportionate number of complaints to inspectors."

This problem occurred when the first tranche of prisoners was transferred and the report concluded it was a problem that needed to be addressed. But I fear that the old bugbear of "doubling up" will linger on even in the modern prison system until any new build prison programme is completed. And the policy of having two communities – sex offenders and run of the mill cons – in one establishment is never going to be without problems. Mind you, it would be naïve to expect the reorganisation of penal affairs in the North-East brought about by the demolition of Peterhead and the building of Grampian not to have hit rough waters at some time or other. Or to have an effect on the penal system in the country as a whole.

The resolution of the dispersal v. concentration argument is interesting in that the authorities ended up putting so much weight on the visiting facilities. Down the years the remoteness from the Central Belt has been a huge disadvantage for Peterhead prisoners of all types, not just the sex offenders. In an interview for a book on his life, TC Campbell, one of two men cleared after years in jail for the Ice Cream Wars murders, said when questioned about the effect the sentence had on his family life: "There was no relationship at all. When I was in Peterhead prison I was only allowed one visit a month that lasted only half an hour and at that time there was no motorway to Peterhead or Aberdeen. There were only country roads and narrow lanes to get there, so my family had to travel 300 miles on bad roads in terrible weather to see me. By the time they got there they were so exhausted that all they could do was sit down and rest. They were not fully rested from their first journey before they were on the road back. I would say that the relationship was torn apart by the whole experience."

But even though the new Peterhead, HMP Grampian, will be a general prison for prisoners from the North-East of Scotland there may well be a few sex offenders in it if they come from that area. Currently approximately half of the sex offender population is located at Glenochil, the rest being distributed throughout other prisons. Actually, it was only about half of the sex offender population that was ever

205

housed at Peterhead anyway, since the sex offender element of the population is around 600 and the most that Peterhead took was 300. The full-scale sex offenders unit is now history. But the role it played in the treatment and rehabilitation, if possible, of such people will not easily be forgotten.

15

THE ESCAPE OF THE BIRD MAN AND
DEATH BY HANGING

As the old prison, totally unfit for purpose as they say, staggered and stuttered to final closure in the dying days of 2013 there was one part of the regime that had improved on the harsh old days of the 1930s. With a couple of interesting exceptions, escapes were a thing of the past. The warning prison bell no longer tolled as frequently as it once did. Governors in the final years slept more peacefully than their predecessors, unworried that a sudden phone call would alert them to an escaper. The good folk in the town and in the countryside around the prison were also less likely to be disturbed by a radio newsflash indicating that it might not be safe to walk the dark streets or open a shed in the garden or search a hayloft in a farm. Actually, only one of the final escapes in Peterhead's history was what a connoisseur of such things would call a proper "over-the-wall" episode. The other could be more accurately described as a prisoner absconding.

The escaper in the late '80s was a guy called Bill Varey, who was a real hard ticket, a military man who, it was rumoured, had been at one time in the legendary French Foreign Legion, not an outfit famed for attracting wimps or shrinking violets. But tough enough for the Legion as he was, big Bill had an unsuspected side to his character – like that famous resident of Alcatraz, Robert Stroud, he had a love of birds. This harmless and seemingly constructive part of Bill's character seemed to pose no threat of escape and the prison authorities positively encouraged his hobby – so much so that he was allowed to build an aviary inside the prison.

Birds, like tropical fish, are judged by some to have a calming influence, though I am not sure you can compare dentists' surgeries with prison. Aviaries are generally constructed of wire and when building one you need to cut wire and to do that it seems obvious that you need wire-cutters. Such tools are self-evidently not a good idea to hand out to enterprising prisoners! But in the case of Birdman Bill the obvious danger of escape was ignored, as the aviary was to be situated behind high wire walls which were themselves encircled by the daunting stone walls of the prison so that the actual chance of escape seemed remote. In any case, the prison officers were around to keep an eye on things.

Varey was tall, fit and strong, but his captors were not hawk-eyed enough to see what was going on and somehow Bill managed to cut a tiny hole in the first fence, and eventually run across the intervening space in the dark and clamber onto the roof of buildings behind the main gate and then scramble across them on to the top of the perimeter wall. There he faced a frightening jump of around thirty feet onto flower beds below. The soft earth of the beds had some cushioning effect. But not enough to prevent him severely

208

damaging an ankle and not long after the daring and clev-
erly contrived escape he was hunted down – something of
a lame duck, you might say – in the Hatton Hotel just a few
miles down the main road south. It was an achievement in
itself to get out but if Bill had any notion of a long spell of
freedom or a return to the Legion he must have been disappointed in that he did not even make it to Aberdeen.

The fact is these days every governor is pretty safe in
assuming that his guests are unlikely to escape when held
in the actual prison. Modern jails with smooth unclimbable
walls, dozens of CCTV cameras, recessed rone pipes and
enough barbed wire to secure a herd of Texas longhorns
are not the easy touch of the old days. And though the
continental criminal classes seem to have a penchant for
helicopters dropping in on prisons and removing thugs
from behind bars, there have been no such aerial spectacu-
lars in Scotland. Though, ironically, one of the most notice-
able things about Peterhead is the almost constant buzz of
the choppers ferrying men and supplies to the North Sea
rigs. Good cover for an enterprising mobster planning an
escape?

Any trip outside jail, for whatever reason, is when the
wily take the chance to do a runner. The story of Thomas
Gordon is a good example.

Gordon was a convicted murderer who escaped from
Peterhead Community Hospital in October 1996. He had
been taken there from the prison for treatment to stab
wounds after an incident in the prison. He managed to slip
away from his guards and was on the run for eleven days
before being recaptured in London. In this he had beaten
the legendary Ramensky, who was generally recaptured a
few miles from the prison.

Gordon's piece of enterprise in giving the two officers who had taken him to hospital the slip was rewarded with a classic "WANTED" poster showing a drawing of him as a dangerous-looking fellow and wording to the effect that he was on the run from prison and should not be approached. It was a dramatic piece of artwork that would not have looked out of place in Dodge City and it is still held in the prison records. But despite its artistic merit, I doubt if its circulation around the Peterhead and Aberdeen areas and the countryside nearby played a role in his recapture when he hid amid the teeming millions of the English capital.

The Varey and Gordon affairs were interesting events in the post-Second World War history of the prison but they do nothing to challenge the record of Gentle Johnny Ramensky as the escaper supreme – he stays at the top of the "over-the-wall" league.

Gordon's escape led to disciplinary action. The senior of the two officers who had taken him to hospital was sacked and took the authorities to court for unfair dismissal. The case dragged on for a couple of years before it was finally ended with a financial out of court settlement. Reinstatement was not deemed to fit the bill in the case of this officer, although the junior officer escaped with a fine of £1,000 and had his period of probation extended.

The previous year had been notable in news terms for the bizarre death by hanging of a serial pervert called Graham Anderson. Anderson, forty-five, was said to be one of the most hated men in the prison, which is saying something. He had ended up "up north" after a series of sex offences. These included exposing himself to young boys and chasing a woman up a street while naked. These particular offences took place just weeks after his release after a sentence imposed for indecent assault. So much for jail as a deterrent!

Always a problem inmate, he was said to have on one occasion tried to castrate himself with a razor blade when in his cell. On the day of his death warders had been concerned about him and burst into his cell to find him partially clothed and hanging with a bin bag over his head. According to a prison source items used in kinky sex games lay near the dangling body. How these objects found their way into a cell is another story but one that seemed to be ignored at the time. It was thought the death was not suicide but a sex game that had gone wrong.

The incident may have been unique in Peterhead but auto-erotic asphyxiation which is aimed at heightening sexual pleasure kills around a hundred or so tormented souls in Britain each year. And it is not a phenomenon confined to prisons. There are many other occasions when people die accidentally this way playing kinky sex games. Notable examples have included politicians and show-business celebrities. No matter, the shock of what the officers found when they entered the cell is another example of the pressure on men and women in the prison service. The hardened cons in the jail at the time had no sympathy for Anderson, indeed they thought that death by hanging was an apt end for such a "monster." It was deemed that it was a fitting way for Anderson to end his existence.

There is a further irony in this hanging in that Peterhead itself was never a place of execution. That infamy belongs to Craiginches prison, also bound for history via the wreckers' ball, at the end of 2013. This was where the last execution in Scotland was carried out. On the morning of 15 August 1963, twenty-one-year-old Henry Burnett took the drop on new gallows specially built in the prison to Home Office specifications. It was the first hanging in Aberdeenshire since 1891. The youngster had at his trial pleaded insanity at the time he had killed a love rival with a shotgun blast full in the face. The court heard of a violent past and attempted suicide. But they only took twenty-five minutes to decide not to accept the claim of insanity or diminished responsibility. After the grim ritual of donning the black cap and the pronouncing of the death sentence both his own family and that of the victim petitioned for a reprieve but Burnett himself, clearly from reports at the time a mixed-up and mentally troubled young man, made no appeal.

So into Craiginches on that summer day stepped hangman Harry Allen, the man who had despatched serial murderer Peter Manuel in the Barlinnie hanging shed five years before. Allen was one of the last to ply his trade and came to prominence in the years after the more famous Albert Pierrepoint had retired after a falling out with the authorities over the size of his fees as a paid killer. Incidentally, in a bizarre change of opinion before he died, Pierrepoint went on record as saying he did not consider hanging a deterrent.

Some of the horror of legal killing is exposed in the tale told about Allen, a cool customer, and his visit to Aberdeenshire. Shortly before escorting Burnett to the gallows and putting a hood over his head then the noose (this sequence was followed to prevent the up draft from the falling body blowing the hood off the head), he lit a cigarette and left it burning in an ashtray. Executions by such as Allen and Pierrepoint were swift and efficient affairs, sometimes taking just a matter of seconds, sometimes less than ten after the victim had been led or dragged into the hanging chamber. After Burnett had disappeared down the trap to eternity Allen was soon back in the holding cell finishing off his cigarette and asking if there was any tea on the go. A sickening little detail of the nature of legal killing.

The Varey and Gordon affairs and the death of Anderson were isolated incidents in the later years when most of the media spotlight and the interest of the public tended to centre on the sex offenders unit and its future. It is interesting that in some way the unit was thought to have contributed to diluting the old wild "Hate Factory" wars, easing the conflict between staff and inmates. In the bad old days the real hard cons let their hatred simmer and then suddenly boil over. One veteran prison officer told me that he believed some of the prisoners took a perverse pride in the place's reputation as the toughest jail in the land. He said some of the guys "needed a good smash-up" every year or so to maintain the prison's top of the league place in the list of hard jails. Some of the officers themselves I suspect took a little secret pride in their status in such a legendary place filled with hard men.

The sex offenders, who despite their perversions were often well educated and intelligent, were well aware that on the outside of the prison bars their vile crimes put them at risk of attack. Likewise inside they were at danger from the ordinary run-of-the-mill cons who had a hatred of what they called "the beasts." Indeed a passport to respect would often be for a straight con to attack a sex offender at any opportunity. Indeed, one infamous US serial killer, Jeffrey Dahmer, was beaten to death by a fellow inmate.

The regular "smash-ups" were a constant nightmare for the prison staff, but they also affected another group – Aberdeen's newspapermen and TV and radio crews. Over the years they spent countless hours at the gates of the old jail. Sometimes they could see the action in front of their eyes as

213

cons tore tiles from the roofs of the cell blocks and hurled them at the warders down below. Or on occasion showing hostages to the press, as in the case of Jackie Stuart who was paraded from the rooftop to underline the danger he was in of being killed by one of his captors. Sometimes the press pack just "doorstepped" the place after a tip-off, patiently waiting for a word or two on what was happening inside. Anyone in the news game in the Aberdeen area knew that the phone could ring any time with a tip-off on some sort of trouble or other in the prison.

The road from the Aberdeen newsrooms north to Peterhead was a familiar and well-worn one. The media men and women reporters met each other regularly in Peterhead and it was at times a sort of team affair, each helping the other since it was impossible for one person to keep on top of what was happening twenty-four/seven. There had to be breaks for sleep, food and drink – they were reporters, after all! The news of what was happening was generally shared. And years back the news was not, as now, packaged by the prison service PR teams. You were not hand-fed by the authorities. You reported what you saw and what information you were getting from contacts built up over years of coverage and familiarity. They still say a reporter is only as good as his contacts, but that was even more the case in the days before mobile phones and laptops and search engines. The North-East press gang were wily and experienced reporters of the best kind.

One word dominates when you talk to the veteran scribblers about these long hours outside the prison – cold. The low temperature and the cutting winds that swept in off the North Sea chilled the reporters to the bone. Holding pencils and notebooks – in the later years laptops – was a nightmare. Ever tried to write with a pair of woollen gloves on? The Thermos and, for some, a wee hip flask with a drop of something warming in it were almost part of a uniform. It is amusing that the press gang still remark on the oddity that somehow or other the prisoners seemed to kick up the most fuss in the cold winter months, maximising the discomfort for the scribblers. And themselves. In Aberdeenshire you would think that anyone planning a day or two on the roof without hot food and warm clothing might pick a summer night for their slate-throwing capers. Not so, the weather was not a factor in their plans.

Another topic within the reporting teams was the fact that when they were wrapped up in gear more suitable for Everest some sturdy North Sea fisherman would stroll past heading for the harbour in shirt sleeves, oblivious to the weather. One man with more memories than most of reporting on the fires, riots, dirty protests, rooftop shenanigans and generally on-going mayhem in the jail is Graeme Smith, who for many years was *The Herald*'s man in Aberdeen. Along with George McDonald he kept readers in Glasgow and Lanarkshire well informed on anything happening in his area. An excellent journalist of the old school – his father was also a legendary North-East newsman – Graeme covered his patch so well that it was a rare occasion when the Glasgow news desk decided to "send" – i.e. give – the men in the north some help from the home office. In practice "sending" usually worked the other way round, with the local expert helping the incomer.

Graeme has now left *The Herald* though he continues to be a major figure in journalism in the area as well as running a public relations operation. He remembers well those cold days outside the prison. One more pleasant memory was

215

of the time TV presenter Lorraine Kelly became a Good Samaritan to the press gang. Lorraine had been sent north to cover one of the major riots and had recourse to the comfort and shelter of the outside broadcast caravan. At frequent intervals she invited the shivering press colleagues in for a wee heat. The girl who had started a glittering career in TV as a reporter on a neighbourhood paper on the outskirts of Glasgow was a real local heroine during these tough days.

Other scribblers and snappers roughed it with less style. Graeme remembers one colleague who bought a fish supper to take to eat in his car at lunchtime only to be called away for some development in the story they were covering. He popped the supper under the seat and returned hours later to scoff it cold. Such interruptions were commonplace – you could spend hours outside the jail or in the local Waterside Hotel, bored and just waiting for something to happen. If eventually you got fed up and decided to go back to the office there would inevitably be a sudden development and you had to return fast. It happened to Graeme many a time. So much so that in long quiet spells his pals would joke Graeme should go home and then the action would start!

If the information on what was going on in these days came not in official statements from the Scottish Prison Service then tip-offs from officers and a pound or two surreptitiously changing hands were an important part of the routine. The stories the press gang covered usually involved violence and serious outbreaks of trouble inside the prison. But there is an old tale of hours being spent trying to find the truth of a rumour that drugs were being smuggled into the jail strapped to the feet of seagulls. As we know, the gulls fly over the walls in search of titbits left by the prisoners, and I suppose it might be technically possible to train one to come regularly to a certain point. It made a good story, but I suspect it was just that. A story.

In the final years the other main media interest was on the political infighting around what would happen now that it was agreed all round that the old place had no future. The options were to pull it down and rebuild it in the same place or to build a new prison on a greenfield site perhaps inland of the town. Or to, as finally happened, close Craiginches as well as Peterhead, disperse the sex offenders and build a new prison to house male and female prisoners and young offenders, in an area adjacent to the existing prison. All the plans had different and varied implications for the locals.

The possibility that the prison in the town would be closed down completely emerged as long ago as 2002 when the then Justice Minister Jim Wallace said that it would indeed close only to make a famous U-turn a few months later after a high-profile campaign led by the wives and partners of prison service officers had secured at least a partial victory. The determined women had to fight for the jail in a way that the prison officers themselves could not – their contracts prevented them talking to the press or taking part in a political action. The women were largely on their own in a fight to the finish with authority and they battled hard and from the heart. It can take a particular kind of man to be a prison officer and wives and partners needed to be a bit special, too. The doughty Peterhead women proved they were up to the challenge.

Amid all the uncertainty about its long-term future the prison still took enormous flak from the HM Inspectorate of Prisons. About the same time as Jim Wallace was making his U-turn a report was issued that spelled out in detail the deficiencies of the prison. An "intermediate" inspection listed a catalogue of complaints. It pointed out that each cell was smaller than the current standard of design and a number of items did not comply with current standards. These included inadequacy of in-cell sanitation, electrical supply to cells, facilities for disabled prisoners, cell call systems, heating and cell windows. It concluded that among other complaints the prison had not been updated to keep abreast of current living standards. It said that "blocks of wood or locally improvised draught excluders were used to fill the gaps left by broken windows, etc."

One reason for this frankly disgraceful state of affairs was jaw-dropping – the budget for capital expenditure on the prison in 2002–03 was £40,000. Compare this with more than £100 million for the building and commissioning of the new HMP Grampian. This dispiriting report went on to say that, "it was difficult to identify parts of the estate that could be described of 'high standard' and of the quality found elsewhere in the SPS estate.

"Office accommodation, work sheds, the condition of the football pitch and staff facilities were all of a poor standard. Despite this, it was encouraging to note that the establishment was exceptionally clean and tidy." Not a happy story with the staff as well as the prisoners suffering from poor conditions. But there was at least to be some physical improvement in the final years, though there was always a reluctance to spend too much on a place on the verge of being demolished.

The fight to ensure a prison stayed in the area went on for years and changed course a few times. Initially the women on the march concentrated on the success of the sex offenders unit, hoping to keep it in the area. They made several compelling points, among them that their menfolk were protecting all of the people of Scotland by keeping paedophiles, rapists and murderers under lock and key. And the wives took every opportunity to point out that their husbands and partners were working with remarkable success, acknowledged worldwide, in trying to turn lives around and prevent reoffending. The sex offenders unit in particular had its work recognised by winning some important awards. But with or without a sex offenders unit it was important for the economic health of the area to keep a prison in the town rather than move it out to, say, Ellon or some other greenfield site.

The campaigners made much of the fact that the option to move out of town had the disadvantage that it would cause much disruption in an area which, unlike Peterhead itself, had not over the years, in quiet times and violent times, learned to live with a prison in the centre of the community. One of the big problems with Peterhead was said to be its remoteness from the Central Belt and the consequent difficulties for visitors to get to the jail. To locate a new prison out in the back country of Aberdeenshire without the travel connections that the fishing community has would just exacerbate the situation. Peterhead is still not the easiest place to get to, but it is easier than travelling to some new prison out in the countryside where there are barely a couple of buses a day.

The campaign organisers also pointed out that the support of the community in Peterhead was of great help to their men who faced such a stressful job. Their neighbours and friends knew well what the prison staff had to deal with. To rebuild the trust Peterhead folk and the jail's workers shared in another more rural place could take years. The campaign organised a petition that showed that

219

the community support was really impressive – more than 17,000 people signed to save the jail. It was not just the ordinary folk of the town that wanted the jail, or a replacement, to stay in the area. The campaign grew to have strong support from local politicians who well understood both the special relationship the communities around the jail had with the prison staff and its commercial value. Indeed Alex Salmond, the Banff and Buchan MP, and Stewart Stevenson MSP were with the campaigners when the petition was handed in. Alex Salmond said that it was a campaign that raised serious issues for all Scots and it was not just about Peterhead. Mr Stevenson said, "The officers at Peterhead do a great job and it is not one that is easy to do. They are recognised throughout the world for their expertise. I believe very strongly that the prison should remain open." He added that there was cross-party support for the wives' campaign, which is "good news."

In the final years it was not just the ageing fabric of the building that demanded change. At some times both Peterhead and Craiginches were at maximum capacity. Indeed at one point Craiginches was overcrowded by 20 per cent, with 263 prisoners shoehorned into a place designed to hold 225. Peterhead was at its maximum of 306. But it was to be several more years after the petition was handed in before the decision was finally taken to build a new prison near the old one which was to be demolished.

The new establishment would have a capacity of around 700. This would make it a super prison in Scottish terms. At the start of the Peterhead story it was pointed out that in the 1880s Scotland was looking over its shoulder to what was happening in England. Again more than 100 years later in the final decision on concentration or dispersal of sex offenders, a lead was taken from what was happening south of the border where the idea of dispersal had firmly won the argument several years earlier.

Now in the days before HMP Grampian finally opens, the debate on the size of new jails is a major penal issue in England – and it looks as if the argument in favour of "super jails" is winning. *The Guardian's* home affairs editor Alan Travis wrote in June 2013 that "more than thirty 'run-down and poorly' located jails, including some of the [English] prison system's most famous names – Dartmoor, Holloway, Pentonville, Wandsworth and Wormwood Scrubs – should be closed down according to prison experts." The main expert in this case is Kevin Lockyer, a former senior Ministry of Justice official and himself an ex-prison governor. He wants to replace "damp Victorian dungeons" with ten to twelve new hub jails holding up to 3,000 inmates.

This plan was opposed by Juliet Lyon of the Prison Reform Trust, who claimed it would be a gigantic mistake to pour money into a "super-sized big-brother prison building drain" and that when it came to prisons the idea that big is beautiful is wrong. She conceded the need to close some outdated prisons but wanted the money saved reinvested into community solutions to crime – though she was not specific what that cumbersome phrase meant. Lockyer, who had produced a report for the right-leaning think-tank Policy Review, expressed a view that could not be more different. He wanted to bust what he called the myth that "small is beautiful."

There is seldom one accepted view on policy when it comes to changes in the prison system. Changes emerge after a slew of argument and counter argument. One of the ideas in the Lockyer report had, to my mind, much to

221

recommend it: the idea that these super jails could contain courts of law. Clearly this would help with the problem of absconding when travelling to and from court and it could save money in transport costs, but maybe it is too radical an idea for politicians. But for the government maybe his estimate that his scheme could produce a saving of £10 billion would be more attractive. The size of the problem in England is illustrated by the fact that a quarter of the 140 prisons there are Victorian or older and a further quarter were built in the 1960s or '70s.

Thankfully the problem in Scotland is not that of the scale in England. Earlier Scotland's First Minister was criticised for calling the old Peterhead a "jewel in the crown" of Scotland's prison service. But that rather extravagant description we could optimistically perhaps apply to its successor.

16

CELL BLOCKS TORN DOWN AND A
FLAG LOWERED ON HISTORY

A visit to Peterhead prison on a sunny spring morning in 2013 when a fresh wind rips through the rigging and flutters the flags of the North Sea supply vessels that throng the completed Harbour of Refuge is a dramatic illustration of how times and places change. On opening more than 100 years ago the old jail, so often described as a grim fortress, presented a far different sight from that of today. Then it stood proud on a headland, the rocks of the bay and the sea to its rear and rolling farmland at its front door. The jail dominated the landscape. To anyone gazing at it, even from some distance off, came the wonder of what it was like behind the iron bars of this Victorian place of imprisonment. No one could tell from the outside what it was like in the hell behind the walls, a permanent hell for inmates and a sometime hell for their jailers. It was, however, obvious to anyone who passed by why the site was chosen – to the rear that cold and roaring North Sea presented any escaper with a huge challenge. Open countryside at the front likewise – it would make any alien figure fleeing in a prison uniform easy to spot.

Today if you did manage to get over the rear walls you would be face to face with security as tight as that in the prison from which you had just fled. On the jail's back door now is a massive storage terminal for the North Sea supply boats drawn to Peterhead by the oil bonanza that began in the 1970s and brought unimagined wealth to the area. Fishing boats are almost outnumbered by the modern gaudy-painted supply vessels – not a whaler in sight – that transport food, drink, spare parts and all the comforts of life needed many miles out to sea on the giant rigs. There is a lot of valuable stuff stockpiled in these offshore yards and it is guarded by high fences, barbed wire and security guards in high-viz clothing. Just like the modern HMP Grampian rising on the ground nearby. Get out the front door of the old jail in 2013 and the escaper would face a different challenge from that of Ramensky in the 1930s. There is a jungle to cross. A jungle of neat little twin-garage bunga-lows, manicured lawns, motor mowers, patio furniture and flower beds. And another jungle of non-stop traffic on the main road from Aberdeen to Fraserburgh. And after that a modern obstacle for someone fleeing inland is to cross a large and busy roundabout, dodging a McDonald's burger bar in the process.

But thoughts of escape were far from my mind when I sat down recently over some ham salad rolls and coffee with Deputy Governor Stuart Campbell and a bunch of long-serving prison officers. The chat was interesting and informative. For instance, I learned that on the closure of the old jail there is talk of producing a special one-off whisky to be sold as a souvenir to staff. There should be no difficulty in sourcing a suitable dram from one of the many nearby Speyside distilleries. This should be superior stuff to that once sold in the Glasgow east end pubs that boasted a label calling its whisky "Barlinnie Bevvy." Any Peterhead dram I suspect would have a bit more class. And though the staff, past and present, might enjoy a wee sip or two chatting about old memories, I doubt if many will shed a tear over the end of the old place. Though one memory many officers told me they would take into retirement or to a new prison in the North-East or down south was that of a strong feeling of camaraderie. A dour Scottish version of real team spirit helped make the dark days bearable. Our chat that day did not need any lubrication. The coffee was enough. Everyone had plenty to say, many memories and forthright views. To Stuart has fallen the daunting task of helping oversee the run down to closure as the previous governor, Mike Hebden, wrestles with any problems thrown up by the building of a new prison next door.

The list of Scottish prison governors who came to the prison service from the military is a long one. The first governor of Peterhead was an ex-army major and the list of his successors is sprinkled with three other majors and, of course, perhaps the most famous of all was the long-serving Captain Buchan, who became so friendly with Johnny Ramensky. It is the same in prisons throughout the land. An army background can be a great advantage. Discipline and leadership are obvious attributes, but it is also true that an army career tends to move a man around many a country and means that in his working life he mixes with humble squaddies and field marshals alike. Good army officers are good motivators, which is a valuable skill in institutions where the depressions and so-called injustices of the inmates can have a knock-on effect on the staff.

The ability to keep calm under fire is also a huge advantage in places like Peterhead, where the missiles heading your way were often slates hurled from a rooftop above. And in a "smash-up," army training can be a lifesaver. Stuart Campbell walks in the footsteps of many a prison service legend. His service was in the artillery and took him to many foreign postings, including Germany. He enjoyed it thoroughly but after eight years it was time to return to Civvy Street and hopefully gainful employment in his local Aberdeenshire area. There was no family connection with the prison service, though that is something that is quite common in jails, but chats with his army mates turned his thoughts to such a career. He applied to Aberdeen with no success but one morning a letter popped through the door and Peterhead was a possible starting place for his prison service career, which also took him to Cornton Vale and Perth and posts in staff training where his old army experience came in particularly handy.

Armies fight wars and in Peterhead in the bad old days towards the end of the last century, as we have heard, there were wars galore. Around 300 prisoners and 200 prison officers were at times like opposing armies. Towards the end of its life Scotland's toughest prison, aka The Hate Factory, had begun to settle down but Stuart Campbell remembers his first introduction to it just days after one of the full-scale riots. Hours before he entered D Hall, where the rioters wreaked havoc and terrorised hostages, it still had police "crime scene" status. To new recruit Stuart it was more like a scene from a Second World War film. From the outside you could see and hear tarpaulins on the roof flapping in the wind, temporarily covering huge holes where the slates had been torn off by rioters and hurled with evil intent at anything that moved below. The halls were three storeys high but so much wreckage – mattresses, smashed tables, chairs, anything that could be torn from its fixings and smashed or burned – had been thrown from the upper floors that the staff had to enter via the first floor. Graffiti was everywhere, scrawled messages saying "screw the bastards" and worse. It was an introduction to life in Peterhead that would not lightly be wiped from the memory of anyone who saw it. The thought must have registered that if the inmates could do this once they could do it again. And they did.

But later riots were less damaging to the fabric of the prison and lessons had been learned the hard way. In particular there are now no attic spaces for rioters to retreat to when pursued by staff. Or to be used as places to hold hostages. The great halls of the prison now in their death throes have clear space under the roof, access to which is prevented by strong steel netting. For anyone taking a last look at the place from outside there are other prominent reminders of lessons learned. The prison is built of huge stone blocks which did not always fit together with extreme accuracy, leaving the small toe and handhold gaps which could be used by good climbers like Ramensky. As you walk down the hill now, past the neat rows of bungalows, to the main reception a glance at the walls shows where light-coloured splashes of cement filling the cracks between blocks stand out against the time-blackened walls. No handholds now for would-be escapers.

As I looked at these smooth smears of cement I remembered years ago Willie "Sonny" Leitch, a one-time Peterhead resident, showing me in a Lanarkshire pub how to use the "cracks" to climb a wall. It was amusing and embarrassing, as the customers must have wondered what this

227

spontaneous masterclass in climbing was all about. Willie knew a thing or two himself about escaping though he never managed it in Peterhead. But in his days in the Royal Navy he had managed to depart a Singapore jail in daring and unauthorised fashion.

Willie, now a reformed and jovial character living in Livingston, is a true prison legend. If he stayed behind the walls in Peterhead he still exercised his sense of humour when there. During a chat with a group of officers one told me of the occasion when Willie, who was a brilliant baker in Civvy Street and who gravitated to the kitchens in prison, heard an approaching party of prison visitors and quickly covered himself in white flour. He then leapt out in front of the visitors appearing as a ghostly figure from the jail's past. Blood pressures were raised! Sonny, now a friend, will not object to me letting you know that he is no Johnny Cash of San Quentin fame when he comes to singing, but he did pen a little ditty himself when he was up north, and again it had a theme that would appeal to all prison inmates:

> Way up on Scotland's North-East coast,
> Just outside Peterhead,
> There stands a grim-grey prison that holds the living dead.
> Bereft of all humanity,
> Devoid of all but pain.
> I hope I never see its inside at any time again.

Sonny tells me that when he put his pen to paper the man in his thoughts was Oscar Slater. It is interesting to note the fascination poetry and folksong-writing has for those behind bars. Willie's friend Walter Norval likes to sing a little ditty he learned in his Glasgow days called the "Barlinnie Hotel" song and he also can recite a rather sad little poetic comment on life in Polmont Borstal called, not surprisingly the "Borstal Song." For a short period the Barlinnie Special Unit had a little magazine called *The Key*, which was an artistic outlet for the desperate men held there. With the likes of Boyle and Hugh Collins around it was naturally strong on drawings of prison life. But the content included a number of dark poems from inmates that were surprisingly good. *The Key*, a rough and ready little compilation held together by staples, was to my mind a really worthwhile exercise but it was not to last long and was killed largely because of opposition from other prison governors. Like much of what went on in that unit it was way ahead of its time.

The flour incident was one of the few touches of humour to emerge from that session of reminiscing during the final days of the prison. Not unnaturally the well documented tales of "batter squads" at the height of the troubles almost fifty years ago were not something these younger men cared to discuss in depth. One intelligent and particularly experienced old hand told me he and other colleagues felt that the public generally did not really understand the provocation that comes from dealing on a daily basis with long-term cons with no hope of release. Nor does the public fully take on the strain of such a job, especially in the bad old days. The newspapers tend to sell copies on the back of lurid tales told by the "bad guys" rather than running insightful features on the worries of the prison staff. This is a common complaint from the officers and if they have a chip on their shoulder, this is it.

I was told of officers who committed suicide not long after entering the service, broken by the demands of the job. The effect on wives and families is also underestimated by the public in the opinion of the staff. It may be that Peterhead will be remembered largely for two different eras – The Hate Factory days and the years of the sex offender unit. The pressure of working in either environment is not something you leave behind when you end a shift. The nature of the job in both regimes puts you in daily contact with the worst in society. When you go home in the evening it is not easy to drop into happy families mode. The work you do stays in your mind, and has an effect on your partner and your children.

In a lighter vein, though, there was also a collective memory of that feeling of camaraderie mentioned earlier. Plenty of memories. Good and bad. One of the good ones is of what must have been some of the most remarkable football matches ever played in Scotland. In the rough pubs on the outside of the prison walls football colours are often banned, the wearing of them considered inflammatory. In such a place the wrong word at the wrong time could easily lead to verbal abuse or in extreme cases the use of weapons – knives now, but not so long ago razors. On the field itself Old Firm matches between Glasgow football rivals Rangers and Celtic were, and still are, no place for the faint-hearted. They attract huge attendances, some of the largest in Britain, and in the clichés of the sportswriters "to retaliate first" and to "take no prisoners" is often the order of the day. The rough and tumble on the park, or a flawed refereeing decision, could spark serious street violence and unrest for hours after a match, whether in the east end of the city or across the river at Govan.

The Glasgow "polis" often made hundreds of arrests on an afternoon of an Old Firm match. Indeed murder was committed on occasion as one side taunted another in the streets. Yet inside Peterhead, which contained some of the hardest of Glasgow hard men, "Old Firm" matches were played without the slightest suggestion of trouble. Mind you, there were only a handful of spectators at these events.

The prisoners vied for selection and put their names down on team lists that mirrored the sectarian divide on the outside. You were either playing for the "Gers" or the "Tic," or the "Huns" or the "Tims," as some would have it. Before and after these matches the prison could talk of little else. They provided a real buzz about the place. But if you had expected the Peterhead Old Firm matches to be a trigger for violence, you would be wrong. They were no games for weaklings and were noted for physicality rather than tactics. But the on-field players could have given their counterparts in the Scottish professional game a lesson or two. The reason was obvious: the cons – both players and spectators – enjoyed the game too much to risk losing it with a rammy or two.

The last governor, in charge during the wind-down, is that remarkable woman Audrey Mooney. She joined the prison service in 1975 and during her career she worked in Cornton Vale, Barlinnie, Shotts and Perth, as well as Aberdeen and Peterhead. Quite a list of service and for it she was awarded an OBE in 2012. On receiving her award she said: "I am extremely proud to have been given this honour and I cannot begin to describe the excitement this has caused my friends and family. This award reflects the fantastic work carried out by all staff in HMPs Aberdeen and Peterhead on a daily basis and I am privileged to work with such a committed and professional group. The opportunity to integrate the work carried out in the prison with partners in the community has been the highlight of a varied and exciting career and I look forward to developing this model to even greater effect."

This was a popular award in the prison community, as there is a feeling that, as pointed out on occasion earlier in this book, the work of those in the prison service can tend to be unnoticed and sometimes unappreciated by the public. Colin McConnell, Chief Executive of the Scottish Prison Service, remarked on that in congratulating Audrey when he said, "To receive an honour is an outstanding recognition for both the individual and the organisation," and he thanked Audrey Mooney on an "immense achievement." So with the bulldozers metaphorically warming up in the background there was some good news around.

The building of the new prison was taking the story onto positive ground. As mentioned earlier, some sections of the community will witter on about luxury and a cushy life – they always do. No new prison anywhere in the world has opened without such criticisms. Even in the Isle of Man, somewhat out of the mainstream on penal matters, the fairly recent opening of a smallish prison exercised writers in the local press to a great extent, filling columns for weeks on end.

What do the opponents of new-build prisons really want – cells with no windows, hammocks, no electric light? Maybe they would go along with the original designers of Peterhead in thinking twice on providing proper sanitation. Would they want to bring back slopping out along with their favourite bee in the bonnet, the return of the rope? Or maybe replace nutritious if unappetising meals with a return to bread and water? It is all about balance, of course. And as comedian Frank Carson used to say, "It's the way you tell them." That is a favourite phrase of newspapermen as well, with regard to the stories that sell their papers, and there is a great truth in it. The spin that compares decent humanitarian conditions to life in "five-star luxury" is all too tempting for a hack under pressure looking to produce an eye-catching headline. The sad basic fact of the convict's loss of liberty is ignored in some sections of society's obsessive prison-bashing.

HMP Grampian has had a taste of this treatment already with the reaction to those stories mentioned earlier of under-floor heating and "toastie toes." A recital of some of the facilities in the new place presented *en masse* will no doubt start the critics off again. The fact is that if we are serious about rehabilitation and cutting reoffending then throwing people into Victorian dungeons miles away from their families to fester for years without hope is not a sensible solution. Think of that penal island in Norway and the success of its regime in getting people out of crime. Without doubt HMP Grampian will not go as far down the road as liberal Norway. But it is a step forward for society that we seem at last to have learned the lesson that treating people like animals does not work at any level. Maybe the Peterhead dirty protests had some effect on the public perception of how prisoners should be treated. Maybe, just maybe, all that aggro thirty years ago edged public opinion a little away from revenge to redemption and rehabilitation.

The "how you tell it" philosophy is illustrated by some of the advance publicity generated by the new prison. A cell is a cell is a cell – a bed, a chair, a window, and toilet and washing facilities and a closed lock on the door – but this to some becomes "en suite rooms with sea views." It is absurd. Down the years football pitches have been a part of prison life. It is a no-brainer to see that the chance for cons to play football and get some of the aggro out of their system is a good idea. In particular the "Old Firm" matches behind bars have proved the beneficial effect of sport and exercise on men imprisoned for years on end. The old Peterhead has goal posts painted on the walls at the end of the exercise yard. The new has, wait for it, "four all-weather football pitches." Is that the end of the world as we know it?

Even the critical point about windows and glimpses of the sea is out of proportion. I remember on a visit to Alcatraz a former inmate telling me of the special sadness brought on at Christmas and New Year by having the ability to be able to look through the bars out across San Francisco and see and hear normal folk enjoying music, drink and fireworks. The windows brought him no comfort and I expect that will be the case in the new prison where the sight of ships arriving and departing and folk as free as birds to go about their daily business may powerfully remind a con he is going nowhere for the next few years.

The new place will also have – shock, horror – landscaped gardens and, here we go again, flat-screen TVs. There will even be a gym, not just a gym but in tabloid speak a gym "that boasts the very best sports equipment." Allotments for the prisoners to work in, too, will be provided. Let them grow veg and admire flowers – whatever next? No matter how much the hangers and floggers dislike it this is likely to be the face of any other new prison built in Scotland.

And there could be quite a few. Barlinnie in particular is ripe for rebuilding. The current governor there, Derek McGill, accepts that the building has outlived its usefulness, as did his predecessor Bill McKinley. Peterhead is lucky that there was space on the doorstep to build a new prison with not too much disruption of the existing place. A powerful driver in any plan to keep a new Barlinnie in the same area of Glasgow rather than go greenfield is what you might say its nearness to its client base. The inmates, by and large, come from the Central Belt and that is a major advantage for visiting and maintaining vital family contacts. To build a new prison on the same site would be difficult, but Derek McGill believes it could be done. The idea would be to temporarily create a rudimentary short-term prison, utilising the sports fields, workshop areas and other spare bits of ground within the walls. After demolition the new prison would rise on the foundations of the old and when it was complete new improved sports, medical and training facilities could be provided after the short-term jail was swept away.

Will it happen? Who knows, but it has been made clear that Grampian will be the first of several new prisons proposed by the Scottish Prison Service. These prisons will be designed to house all categories and age groups of prisoners, both male and female. The new-style prisons will be unique in the UK. On a visit to examine progress on the site, Scottish Justice Minister Kenny MacAskill commented on how the Scottish Prison Service would generally benefit from the example of the new prison. He said it was a very exciting development and Scotland's first custom-built "community-facing prison," in this case one designed to meet the custodial needs of the North-East. He went on: "As well as helping to develop a model which I believe will be the future for our custodial services, it will mean prisoners from the North-East will be able to benefit from facilities specifically designed to reduce their offending. The new fit for purpose facilities will maximise the opportunity for prisoners to engage positively to address the underlying causes of their offending behaviour."

One of the major tests facing the Scottish Prison Service will be getting the public on side with regard to the new thinking that comes with new prisons. Already there is a lot of evidence that this will not be easy. Look at the flack already directed at the prison even during the building period. But speaking to Mike Hebden, the man who will be part of the top management team at HMP Grampian when it finally opens its doors in 2014, I was struck by his positive attitude on what lay ahead when the old prison is turned to dust and only the memories of the iconic jail remain.

He told me: "My association with Peterhead prison goes back to 1989, when I joined the SPS as an officer, and in the intervening twenty-four years I have returned to the establishment a further three times as my career has progressed, culminating in having the privilege of being governor in charge of the prison between 2010 and 2012.

"During my service at Peterhead I experienced a range of different prisoner types and related regimes; from the post-riot 'lock-down' regimes of the late '80s and early '90s, through the innovative, groundbreaking introduction of sex offender treatment programmes from the mid-1990s and on to the change to a local, short-term prisoner population in 2012.

"There have been good times and not so good times but the common thread throughout all of my experience of Peterhead has been the skill, professionalism and dedication of the staff group who have worked there; rising to and meeting the challenges and opportunities which the various regime changes have required and providing a significant contribution to making Scotland a safer place for us all to live in.

"Looking forward, as a Peterhead 'loon' myself, I take great pleasure in knowing that the town's association with and support of the Scottish Prison Service will continue into the future through the creation of HMP & YOI Grampian; and having been involved in the design and development of the new prison from its conception, I am confident that it will provide a state-of-the-art facility which will facilitate the continuation of this important work.

"So as I bid farewell to Peterheid (or 'the Napper' as it is affectionately known throughout SPS), it is in the knowledge that a new generation of prison staff will continue to serve their community within this new facility, in the same positive manner that the 'Warders' who preceded them over the last 125 years have done."

It was a well-expressed and realistic final tribute to the men and women who served in the Napper. When the prison's Saltire is finally lowered on history and a new one hoisted at HMP Grampian, a new era begins. What will the future hold? Who knows? That is another story. But I doubt if it will have the twists and turns, dramas and tragedies, successes and failures of the place once known infamously as The Hate Factory. The place that was Scotland's toughest prison.

APPENDIX

THE GOVERNORS

Major S. A. Dodd, 1888–1908
Major F. H. D. Playfair, 1908–1908
J. Stewart, 1908–1923
Major R. E. W., 1923–1930
Captain J. I. Buchan, 1930–1950
Major D. C. Herron-Watson, 1950–1958
D. Mackenzie, 1958–1961
J. Frisbie, 1961–1964
A. Angus, 1964–1969
R. Hendry, 1969–1974
W. Gardener, 1974–1976
A. K. Gallagher, 1976–1979
G. Dingwall, 1979–1981
A. Smith, 1981–1988
A. Coyle, 1988–1990
M. Milne, 1990–1991
A. Spencer, 1992–1996
W. A. R. Rattray 1996–2001
I. D. F. Gunn, 2001–2006
A. Mooney, 2007–2008
M. Stoney, 2009–2010
M. T. Hebden, 2010–2012
A. Mooney, 2012–Present

INDEX

241